Mel Bay Presents

A Co...

GUIDE

TO Musical Terms

by John Robert Brown

To Celia
— Colleague and friend.
All good wishes
John Robert Brown
March 2003

1 2 3 4 5 6 7 8 9 0

Visit us on the Web at www.melbay.com — E-mail us at email@melbay.com

John Robert Brown, compiler of 'A Guide to Musical Terms', is a saxophonist, clarinetist and author. His professional playing experience ranges from membership of a 'sixties Hamburg rock group to occasional work with the Hallé Orchestra. He is the author of *How to Play Saxophone* and *La Clarinette Sans Professeur*. He contributed a chapter to *The Cambridge Companion to the Clarinet*, drew pencil portraits for *The Cambridge Companion to the Saxophone*, writes a *Reed Clinic* column for the magazine *Crescendo International*, and contributes to *CASS Magazine*, the journal of the Clarinet and Saxophone Society of Great Britain.

Currently John Robert Brown is External Relations Consultant for Leeds College of Music, Britain's largest music conservatory. In this capacity he travels worldwide.

Of size and style to slip easily into a pocket or instrument case, these pages contain most terms that will be met by musicians in the classroom, rehearsal room or recording studio. There are also many definitions of historical interest.

My thanks to my German friend Lydia Laxy for advice about her native language.

John Robert Brown

Key to languages, abbreviations, meanings of italics, etc.

Eng = English
F   = French
G   = German
It   = Italian
L   = Latin
P   = Portuguese
Sp   = Spanish

Where terms are from Greek, Norwegian, etc., the name of the language is given in full.

Terms written in *italics* appear with their own entry.

Bold capital letters are used to spell out abbreviations - thus: **B**inary Dig**IT**, **M**echanical **C**opyright **P**rotection **S**ociety.

Foreword

This book, intended both for the general public as well as musicians of all ages, provides a unique dictionary of musical terms and expressions.

John Robert Brown, a colleague and friend of mine for many years, has given us here an invaluable compendium of the terms and words most frequently encountered in classical, jazz and popular music. Essential expressions, instructions and technical messages from a variety of languages are defined within these pages in a reference book which combines clarity and precision with scholarly insight. This comprehensive guide in a convenient pocket format will fulfil a vital role for the widest possible range of readers.

We would like to express our gratitude to William Bay and all his staff at Mel Bay Publications, Inc. for making this book and this series possible. We must also thank Elizabeth Wade for editorial assistance during the preparation of the work.

Graham Wade
General Editor, ALL ABOUT MUSIC SERIES

A

a (It), **à** (F) At, by, for, with, in, to, in the manner of.

A and R Artists and Repertoire. A record company employee responsible for performers and their material.

ab (G) Off. From…onwards.

abandonné (F) Negligent, (i.e. freely).

a battuta (It) With the beat.

abbandono (It) Abandon, (free, passionate).

abbassare (It) To lower, to tune down a (stringed) instrument to obtain a note normally out of range.

abbellimenti (It) Embellishments.

abbellire (It) To embellish with ornaments.

abdämpfen (G) 'To damp off'. To mute.

Abend (G) Evening.

Abendlied (G) Evening song.

aber (G) But.

Abgang (G) Exit (off stage).

abgestossen (G) See *abstoßen*.

ab initio (L) From the beginning.

ablösen (G) To loosen from one another, e.g. to play *staccato* (separate the notes), to take the finger off.

abnehmend (G) 'Off-taking', 'taking away' (of tone). Decreasing. *Diminuendo*.

aboio (P) Wordless song used by Brazilian cowboys, to call cattle.

ABRSM The Associated Board of the Royal Schools of Music. A British commercial music-publishing company and examining body, operating internationally.

abruzzese (It) A song or dance in the style of the Abruzzi district, to the east of Rome.

Abschiedssymphonie (G) Farewell Symphony. Symphony No. 45 in F sharp minor, composed 1772, Haydn.

absetzen (G) To play detached. See *ablösen*.

absolute music The opposite of *program music*, music without any external associations.

absolute pitch The ability to immediately sing the pitch of any note asked for, or to recognize any note heard. Also called *perfect pitch*.

absolutes Gehör (G) *Absolute pitch, perfect pitch.*

abstoßen (G) To detach notes from one another, to play *staccato*.

Abstrich (G)

abwechseln,
abzuwechseln (G)

acalento (P)
a cappella (It)

a cappella (jazz)

a capriccio (It)
accarezzevole,
accarezzevolemente (It)
accelerando, accel. (It)
accent
accentato (It)
accento (It)
accentué (F)
acciaccato (It)
acciaccatura (It)

accidental

accompagnato (It)
accompaniment

accoppiare (It)
accoppiato (It)
accord (F)
accordare (It)
accordatura (It)
accorder (F)
accordion

In organ playing, to cease to use a stop.
Down - bow.
To exchange. Instruction to a player to change instruments.
Lullaby from Portugal.
'Chapel'. Used to describe choral music that is composed to be sung unaccompanied.
Used to describe a passage in a (jazz) orchestration where the *front line* instruments are scored to play without the rhythm section. A feature of the jazz orchestra work of Thad Jones, Bob Florence and others.
Capriciously.
Caressing, caressingly.

Gradually getting faster.
To emphasize or stress a note.
Accented.
Accent.
Accented.
Broken down, crushed.
A short *grace note* played almost simultaneously with the principal note, and released immmediately.
A sign (*sharp, flat, double sharp, double flat, natural*) indicating a temporary departure from the key signature. It holds good only for the duration of the measure in which it appears. In complex passages a reminder may appear in brackets, a courtesy accidental.
Accompanied.
Supporting part for an instrumental or vocal performance.
To couple (organ).
Tied.
1. Chord. **2.** Tuning.
To tune.
Tuning.
To tune.
A portable instrument, usually strapped across the chest, in which a hand-operated bellows pushes air across a metal reed. The air is released by valves controlled either by a piano-style keyboard, or by buttons.

accoupler (F)	To couple (organ).
accusé, accusée (F)	Emphasized.
acetate (jazz)	A form of sound recording (etching onto acetate plastic), fragile and not durable, used as a preliminary sample during the recording process. Current during the 78 and vinyl eras, no longer used.
acht (G)	Eight.
Acht (G)	Care.
Achtel, Achtelnote (G)	Eighth note. *Quaver*.
Achtelpause (G)	Eighth note rest. *Quaver rest*.
achtstimmig (G)	In eight voices or parts.
Achtung! (G)	Attention! Stand by!
Achtung Anfänger (G)	Beginners please.
acid house	Type of popular music, with a pulse of 120-135 beats per minute, that blends house music with the drug Ecstasy, otherwise known as acid.
acid jazz	Hybrid jazz equivalent to *acid rock*.
acid rock	Highly amplified music popular between the late 1960s and the 1980s. A forerunner of *heavy metal*. Acid refers to LSD (Lysergic Acid Diethylamide-25), drug used by many rock performers.
acoustics	The science of sound.
action	**1.** The distance between the strings and the *fingerboard* or *fretboard* on a string instrument. **2.** The actuating mechanism of an instrument.
active loudspeaker	A loudspeaker containing its own amplification circuitry.
adagietto (It)	Rather slow, but faster than *adagio*.
adagio (It)	Slow. 'At ease'. A tempo between *andante* and *largo*.
added sixth	A *triad* with the sixth added.
additive synthesis	Synthesizing sound by combining *sine waves* of different frequencies and amplitudes.
addolcendo (It)	Becoming *dolce*.
addolorato (It)	Grieved, sadly.
Adel (G)	Nobility.
Adeste Fideles (L)	O Come, All Ye Faithful. A Latin hymn.
à deux, à 2, (F)**, a due, a 2** (It)	Divided between two instruments or voices, or an instruction for two instruments to join in playing the same line of music.
adiaphonon	An early tuning-fork piano.
adirato (It)	Angered, irate.

adjunct	Word used to describe notes that are 'inessential' to the harmony, e.g. *passing notes.*
ad libitum, ad lib. (L)	At choice. Meaning either that the passage may be performed freely, or that an instrument in a score may be omitted. In jazz scores, it indicates that the soloist is to improvise.
ADSR	Attack, Decay, Sustain, Release. In *synthesis*, the parameters normally comprising an *envelope.*
a due corde (It)	On two strings.
Aeolian harp	A string instrument comprising a resonant chamber (usually a form of wooden box) with gut strings attached. This is hung out of doors and the blowing of the wind vibrates the strings.
Aeolian mode	A *mode* whose pattern of notes is the same as playing A to A on the white keys of the piano. Also called the *natural minor* scale.
affabile (It)	Affable.
affaiblissant (F)	Weakening. *Diminuendo.*
affannato (It)	Panting. In a distressed manner.
Affekt (G)	Fervor.
affetto (It)	Affection.
affettuoso (It)	Tenderly.
affezione (It)	Affection.
affrettando, affret. (It)	Hurrying.
affrettare (It)	To hurry.
afoxê (P)	*Cabaca.*
Afro-Cuban jazz	Jazz style from the 1940s, fusing *bop* (*bebop*) with traditional Cuban elements.
afterbeat	Any beat of the bar other than the *downbeat.*
aftertouch	The introduction of electronic *modulation* (*vibrato*, etc.) to notes already playing by using a touch or pressure facility incorporated into a keyboard.
agevole (It)	Comfortable.
aggiustamente (It)	Adjusting.
aggradevole (It)	Agreeable.
agiatamente (It)	Comfortably, freely.
agilement (F)	In an agile manner.
agilmente (It)	In an agile manner.
agitato (It)	Agitated.
agité (F)	Agitated.
agogic accent	An emphasis placed on a note by making it longer than normal.
agogô (P)	Double cowbell. Each bell is a different size.

ähnlich (G)	Similar.
ai (It)	At the, to the.
aigu, aiguë (F)	Shrill, high in pitch.
air	Melody.
air check	During the 78 rpm era in America, the recording of a radio broadcast.
air guitar	An imaginary guitar.
Ais (G)	The note A sharp.
aise (F)	Ease.
Aisis (G)	The note A double sharp.
Akkord (G)	*Chord.*
Akt (G)	Act.
al, alla (It)	To the, in the manner of.
à la pointe (F)	Use the *bow* of a string instrument at the point, (at the end opposite to that held by the player).
Alberti bass	A bass figure using broken chords, named after Domenico Alberti (c.1710-1740), whose composition style made much use of this device.
alborada (Sp)	*Aubade.* Morning song.
album	Originally a collection of 78 rpm records, presented like a book - hence 'album'. Later transferred to describe a full-length *vinyl* LP recording.
Albumblatt (G)	A page or leaf from a book. A short simple piece.
al coda (It)	To the *coda.*
aleatoric music	Music in which chance is used to determine important parameters.
al fine (It)	To the end.
alla breve (It)	With a half note (*minim*) beat, and usually implying a faster tempo.
alla marcia (It)	In the style of a march.
alla misura (It)	In strict time.
allant (F)	Going, getting. Moderately slowly.
allargando (It)	Broadening. Becoming slower, and usually louder.
alle (It)	To the.
allegramente (It), **allégrement** (F)	Brightly, gaily.
allegretto (It)	Fairly quick, but not quite as quick as *allegro.*
allegrezza (It)	Mirth, cheerfulness.
allegro (It)	Quick. Literally 'cheerful'.
allein (G)	Alone.
allemand (F)	German.

allemande (F)

The name of two types of composition:
1. Also called almain, alman, almand. As found in the classical *suites* of Bach, Handel and others. Unless preceded by a *prelude*, the allemande opens the suite. Of serious but not heavy mood, the speed is moderate, a typical allemande has four beats to the measure, in *binary* form. Each half opens with a short note at the end of a measure.
2. The contemporary allemande, still danced in parts of Germany and Switzerland, is in triple time, and lively.

allentamento,
allentando (It)

Slowing, slowed.

allmählich (G)

Gradually.

allonger (F)

To lengthen, to slow down.

allora (It)

Then.

all' ottava (It)

An *octave* higher.

allure (F)

Gait, manner.

alphorn, alpenhorn

A long wooden horn, from Switzerland. Made of wood, curved slightly, with an upturned bell.

als (G)

Than. When. As.

al segno (It)

To the sign.

als möglich (G)

As possible.

alt, altered (chord) (jazz)

Dominant seventh chord with chromatically altered extensions. The symbol *G7(alt)* describes a chord containing G, B, D, F, Ab, Bb.

alt (It)

High. In vocal music *in alt* refers to notes in the octave above the treble stave, starting with G; *in altissimo*, in the octave above that.

alternate fingering

False fingering.

Altgeige (G)

Viola.

altissimo (It)

Very high.

alto

'High'. Properly still applied to the highest (adult) male voice. The real alto is today so rare that it has become common to speak of contraltos as altos, and publishers' catalogs now indicate 'SATB.' (Soprano, Alto, Tenor, Bass) rather than 'SCTB.'

alto (F)

Viola.

alto clef

The C clef falling on the center (third) line of the staff, used almost exclusively by the *viola.*

alto flute

Lower version of the transverse *flute*, pitched in G.

alto saxophone

Member of the *saxophone* family pitched in Eb.

alto trombone

A high *trombone*, its range approaching that of the

	trumpet. Obsolete. Parts for this instrument are now played on the tenor trombone.
Altposaune (G)	*Alto trombone.*
altro, altra (It)	Other.
AM	*Amplitude Modulation.*
am (G)	At the, on the, to the, by the, near the.
amabile (It)	Amiable, pleasant, lovable.
amarevole, amarezza (It)	Bitterly, bitterness.
amen cadence	*Plagal cadence.* Progression from chord IV to chord I.
am Frosch (G)	Use the bow at the *heel* (literally *at the frog*).
amore (It)	Love.
amoroso (It)	Loving.
amour (F)	Love.
amp (jazz, rock)	*Amplifier.* Frequently used to describe speaker and amplifier combination. See *sound reinforcement.*
ampleur (F)	Breadth.
amplifier	Electronic sound reinforcement.
amplitude	In *synthesis*, the height of a wave. This corresponds to the loudness of the sound.
amplitude modulation	In *synthesis*, the periodic alteration of the volume of an *audio* signal to produce effects such as *tremolo.*
am Steg (G)	Bowing on the *bridge.*
an (G)	On, by, to, at.
anacrusis (pl. **anacruses**)	Pick up, or lead in, (unstressed) at the beginning of a phrase or start of a piece.
analog (**analogue**)	In *synthesis*, the use of voltages to control *amplitude, pitch,* and *timbre.*
analysis	The study of the form and structure of music.
anapest, anapaest	A poetical or musical 'foot', consisting of two short syllables or notes, and one long one.
anche (F)	*Reed.* Reeds, on organ.
anche (It)	Also.
ancora (It)	Repeat, still, yet.
Andacht (G)	Devotion.
andamento (It)	An unusually long *fugue* subject.
andante (It)	Going. At a walking pace.
andantino (It)	Slightly faster than *andante.*
andauernd (G)	Lasting, (continuing).
ander, andere (G)	Other.
an der Spitze (G)	Use the bow at the point.
anechoic	Without echo.

Anfang (G)	Beginning.
angemessen (G)	Suitable to.
angenehm (G)	Agreeable, pleasant.
anglais, anglaise (F)	English.
angore (It)	Pain, anxious wish.
angoscia (It)	Anguish.
angreifen (G)	To seize hold, to attack.
Angst (G)	Anguish, anxiety, fear.
ängstlich (G)	Anxious, uneasy.
anhalten (G)	To hold on. Sustain.
Anhang (G)	Appendix, supplement.
anima (It)	Soul, spirit. *Con anima* means 'with feeling'.
animando (It)	Becoming more lively.
animato (It), **animé** (F)	Animated, lively.
animo, animoso (It)	Spirit, spirited.
anlaufen (G)	To increase the sound, *crescendo*.
Anmut, (Anmuth) (G)	Grace.
anreissen (G)	To use strong *pizzicato*. To tear at.
Ansatz (G)	The *embouchure* in wind playing. The *attack* in vocal or string playing.
Anschlag (G)	Attack, touch.
anschlagen (G)	To play. *So leise als möglich anschlagen* = play as gently as possible.
anschmiegend (G)	Bent to, shaped to, compliant.
ansia (It)	Anxiety.
anstatt (G)	Instead of.
anstimmen (G)	To tune. To give a *keynote*. To start singing.
Anstrich (G)	Stroke of a *bow*.
answer	In a *fugue*, the second entry of the *subject*.
antecedent	The first phrase of a musical *period*. The *subject* of a *fugue*.
anthem	A choral composition, written in English for performance in a church.
anticipation (jazz)	Playing (intentionally) in front of the beat. In band arrangements the tension, and swing, may be increased by moving the melody (and the associated harmonic change) one or two beats forward.
antico, antica (It)	Antique, ancient.
antiphonal, antiphony	Call and *answer*.
Antwort (G)	Answer, fugal answer.
anvil	An orchestral percussion instrument imitating a real anvil.

12

anwachsend (G)	Growing.
Anweisung (G)	Stage direction.
anzublasen (G)	To be blown.
Aolsharfe (G)	*Aeolian harp.*
AOR	Album Orientated Rock. Categorization used by record companies and radio stations.
apaisé (F)	Calmed.
à peine (F)	Hardly, barely.
aperto (It)	Open. Clear, distinct. With the bell unstopped.
a piacere (It)	At pleasure. The performer is free to depart slightly from the written rhythm.
apito (P)	Whistle. Samba whistle.
appassionato (It)	With passion.
appena (It)	Hardly, scarcely, slightly.
appenato (It)	Pained, tormented.
appoggiando (It)	Leaning, leaned.
appoggiatura (It)	An accented non-chord note that resolves stepwise to a chord note. Literally 'leaning'.
a punta d'arco (It)	With the point of the bow. See *à la pointe.*
arabesque (F)	A florid melodic style. 'Arabian'.
arada (Sp)	A folk song genre, associated with ploughing in Spain.
arbitrary minor scale	*Melodic minor scale.*
arcata (It)	Stroke of the bow.
arcato (It)	Bowed.
archet (F), **archetto** (It)	Bow.
archlute	A *lute* with two pegboxes.
archtop guitar	A *guitar* with an arched top, and *f* holes. Used in *jazz.*
arco (It)	*Bow.* With the bow. Normally an instruction after *pizzicato.*
ardemment (F)	Ardently.
ardente (It)	Ardent.
ardito (It)	Bold.
ardore (It)	Ardor.
aria	Air. A solo vocal piece within an *opera* or *oratorio.*
arietta (It), **ariette** (F)	A shorter and simpler *aria.*
arioso (It)	**1.** *Recitative.*
	2. A synonym for *cantabile.*
	3. A melodic passage at the beginning or end of a *recitative.*
	4. Any short air in an *opera* or *oratorio.*

arlecchinesco (It)	Harlequinesque.
armonia (It)	Harmony, wind band.
armonica	Early spelling of *harmonica*, meaning musical glasses, not *mouth organ*.
armonioso, armoniosamente (It)	Harmonious, harmoniously.
arpa (It)	*Harp.*
arpège (F)	*Arpeggio.*
arpeggiare (It)	Spread the notes of a chord, from the bottom upwards. Like a harp.
arpeggio (It)	Notes of a chord played in succession, 'harp-like'. A broken chord.
arpeggione (It)	A type of *cello*, shaped like a guitar, played with a bow and fretted. *Guitare d'amour.*
arraché (F)	Torn.
arrangement	The setting, reworking, reharmonizing or recomposing of a musical composition.
ars antiqua (L)	Old Art. See *ars nova.*
arsis (Greek)	Upbeat.
ars nova (L)	New Art. Term coined at the beginning of the fourteenth century to mark a general freeing of style from the old influences of *organum*.
articolato (It)	Well articulated.
articulation	The degree to which notes are separated or connected. A synonym for *tonguing* in wind playing.
articulé (F)	Well articulated.
artig (G)	Well-behaved.
As (G)	The note A flat.
ASCAP	**A**merican **S**ociety of **C**omposers, **A**uthors and **P**ublishers. An American copyright and performing right organization.
askaulos	An ancient Greek name for the *bagpipe*.
aspiratamente (It)	Aspiringly.
aspro, aspra (It)	Rough, harsh.
assai (It)	Very, extremely. See *assez.*
assez (F)	Enough, sufficiently. (Sometimes used in the same sense as *assai*.)
assieme (It)	Together.
Assistent (G)	Assistant stage manager.
Associated Board	**A**ssociated **B**oard of the **R**oyal **S**chools of **M**usic (*ABRSM*). A British commercial examining institution, operating worldwide.

assoluto (It)	Absolute.
atabaque (P)	Generic Brazilian name for conical single-headed drums played with the hands. Similar to Cuban *conga drum*.
Atem (G)	Breath.
Atempause (G)	Breath pause.
a tempo (It)	In time; at the previous speed.
atmosphere microphone	Microphone used to pick up audience noise or other ambient sound.
atonal	Music without a key center.
attacca (It)	Go on at once, usually to the next section of music. See *segue*.
attacco (It)	A short *motif* used for imitation in *counterpoint*.
attack	The start of a note. To begin (a note) forcibly.
attack time	The time taken for a sound to reach maximum loudness from silence.
attaque (F)	Attack.
attenuator	In *synthesis*, the device controlling the level of a signal.
au (F)	To the, at the.
aubade (F)	Early morning music. See *alborada*.
auch (G)	Also.
audace (F), (It)	Audacity. Audacious.
au dessous (F)	Beneath, less than.
audio	Electronic sound treatment or reproduction.
audition	Hearing. A performance given to determine college entrance, or the award of a performing position or prize.
auf (G)	On.
aufführen (G)	To perform.
Aufführung (G)	Performance.
Aufführungspraxis (G)	Performance practice.
aufgeregt (G)	Excited.
aufgeweckt (G)	Wakened up, lively.
aufhalten (G)	To hold up, to retard.
Auflage (G)	Edition.
auflösen (G)	To loose, to untie. To resolve a *discord*.
Auflösungszeichen (G)	*Natural*. 'Release sign'.
Aufschlag (G)	Upbeat.
Aufschnitt (G)	Slit, slice. Thus, a cut.
Aufschwung (G)	Up-soaring, flight. In a lofty spirit.
Aufstrich (G)	Up-stroke (of a bow).
Auftakt (G)	Upbeat.

auftreten (G)	To enter, to appear on stage.
Auftritt (G)	Scene, (stage) entrance.
Aufzug (G)	Act (noun).
augmentation and diminution	The lengthening and shortening of the time-values of a melody. This term is usually encountered in the discussion of *fugue* subjects.
augmented fourth	Interval of six half-steps or semitones, using four letter names, e.g. C to F sharp, or G to C sharp.
augmented interval	A major or perfect interval raised by a half-step.
augmented sixth chord	Name given to *French sixth*, *German sixth* and *Italian sixth* chords, where the interval of an augmented sixth resolves outwards to an octave.
augmented triad	A triad comprising two major thirds, e.g. C, E, G sharp, or F, A, C sharp.
aulos	Ancient Greek double reed instrument.
aura (It)	*Jew's harp.*
aural training	Ear training. Learning the ability to recognize, name or write down music heard.
aus (G)	Out of, from.
Ausdruck (G)	Expression.
Ausgabe (G)	Edition.
Ausgang (G)	Exit (of building).
ausgehalten (G)	Held out, sustained.
ausgewählte (G)	Selected.
aushalten (G)	To hold out, to sustain.
ausschlagen (G)	To beat out, to beat time.
ausser (G)	Out of, in addition to. Except.
äusserst (G)	Extremely.
aussi (F)	Also, as much, therefore.
Aussprache (G)	Pronunciation.
Ausstattung (G)	Design.
Auszug (G)	Arrangement, reduction, extract. Departure, exodus.
au talon (F)	Use the bow (of a string instrument) at the *heel*, i.e. at the end held by the player.
autoharp	A type of *zither*. Chords are played on it by strumming. Those strings which are to remain silent are damped by pads operated by *keys*.
autre, autres (F)	Other, others.
auxiliary note	A type of *passing note* which does not move on, but returns to where it started. A passing note that has lost its nerve.
AV	Audio-Visual.

16

avant (F), **avanti,**
avante (It)

Before, preceding, forward.

avec (F)

With.

Ave Maria (L)

Hail Mary.

axe (jazz)

Slang (1950s jazz) term for instrument (see also *horn*).

azione (It)

Action, drama.

B

B, b (G)   The note or key B♭ in German.

b   In guitar tablature, bend string up.

baby grand   A small grand piano, for domestic use.

Bacchanalia   Wild celebration in honor of the god of wine, Bacchus.

bacchetta (It)   Stick, drumstick, *baton*.

Bach trumpet   A valveless trumpet, in C or D. Often believed to be the valveless trumpet of Bach's day, but originally (c.1884) a straight trumpet in A with two valves.

backbeat   Heavy emphasis of beats two and four in *common time*.

backing track   A recorded accompaniment.

back line   Sound reinforcement and other equipment, which is placed behind (at the back of) the musicians, hence the term.

badinage, badinerie (F)   Playfulness, trifling. The name of a dance movement of a *suite*.

baffle   1. A piece of studio equipment, usually a large (padded) portable board, used in a recording studio to deaden or divert sound.
                      2. The part of the inside of a clarinet or saxophone mouthpiece opposite the reed.

bagatelle (F)   Trifle.

bagpipe   Reed-pipe instrument, with the air supply stored in a bag. The air supply may be from the mouth (as in the Scottish Highland pipes) or filled by bellows under the player's arm (as in the Northumbrian pipes).

baguette (F)   Drumstick. Also *baton*, and the name of the wood of a bow.

baile, bayle (Sp) Generic name for Spanish dances of Moorish origin.

baisser (F)   To lower.

baixo (P)   Bass.

baixo profundo (P)   Deep bass.

balalaika   A triangular-bodied Russian *guitar*, with *frets* and three strings. See also *domra*.

balance   The adjustment of volume and blend between performers. It can refer to live performance, or to the effect when recorded or broadcast.

balancement (F)	*Tremolo.*
baldamente (It)	Boldly.
Balkon (G)	Gallery.
ballabile (It)	In a dance style.
ballad	**1.** A simple song.
	2. In popular music or jazz, a love song in a slow tempo.
	3. A traditional song that tells a story.
ballade (F)	A name first used by Chopin, for a lyrical instrumental piece.
balladenmässig (G)	In ballad style.
ballet	Theatrical dance form, with sets and music.
Ballett (G)	*Ballet.*
balo	A gourd-resonated frame *xylophone* of West Africa.
bamboula	*Tambourine.*
Band, Bände (G)	Volume, volumes. (Book.)
bandola (Sp)	A Spanish string instrument, similar to the *lute.*
bandolim (P)	*Mandolin.*
bandoneon	German type of *concertina* named after its inventor, Heinrich Band. The instrument takes a leading role in Argentinian tango bands.
bandora	*Pandora.*
bandurria (Sp)	A type of Spanish *guitar*, with six double strings.
banjo	Fretted string instrument of American origin, the body of which is a round drum covered by a vellum or plastic head.
banjulele	A version of the *ukulele,* having a round *banjo* type body.
baqueta (P)	Drumstick.
bar, bar line	*Measure.* The space between two bar lines, or the bar line itself.
barber shop music	Originally vocal music sung by an all-male quartet (TTBB). Characterized by a harmonic style wherein the melody is in the second voice. Said to have originated in nineteenth century barber shops.
barcarolle	Boat song, supposedly derived from songs of Venetian gondoliers, and usually in 6/8 or 12/8 time.
bariolage (F)	'Motley coloring'. In violin playing, a rapidly repeated shifting from a stopped string to an open string. A device brought to guitar playing by Charlie Christian.

baritone	Male singing voice between tenor and bass.
Barkarole (G)	*Barcarolle.*
bar line	In written music, the vertical line that marks out *measures* or bars.
Baroque	The musical era that lasted from c.1600-1750.
barre (F)	Bar. Term used by guitarists and lutenists to mean a finger laid across two or more strings at one fret.
barrelhouse	A style of early jazz piano playing, a forerunner of *boogie-woogie*, but four in a measure. Term also used to mean 'rough' or 'crude'.
barrel organ	Portable automatic organ, with an action similar to a *musical box*. Usually cranked by hand.
bas (F)	Low.
bass	1. The lowest male singing voice.
	2. The lowest instrument.
	3. The lowest part of the music.
	4. The double bass.
bass clef	The common name of the F clef, having the F below middle C on the highest line but one.
bass drum	A very large double-headed drum used in orchestras and bands. Also the largest drum in the kit used in jazz and rock combos.
basse chiffrée (F)	*Figured bass.*
basse continue (F)	*Figured bass.*
basset horn	Alto clarinet.
bass fiddle	*Double bass.*
Baßgeige (G)	*Double bass.*
bass guitar	A fretted bass instrument with a solid body, and thus acoustically silent and requiring amplification. It is tuned an octave lower than the guitar, and usually has four strings.
Baßklappenhorn (G)	*Ophicleide.*
basso continuo (It)	*Figured bass.*
basson quinte (F)	*Tenoroon.*
bassoon	Low *double reed* woodwind instrument.
bateria (P)	Drums.
baton	Conductor's stick.
batonka	An arrangement of plastic drainpipes used as a percussion instrument.
batterie (F)	The noisier percussion instruments.
battre (F)	To beat.
battuta, battute (It)	Beat, beats. *A battuta* means 'in strict time'.

batucada (P)	Drumming session or percussion playing involving different instruments.
batuco	Music from Cape Verde Islands. See also *finaon*.
Baumwollschlegel (G)	Cotton stick (percussion).
B dur (G)	Key of B major.
Be (G)	The sign ♭.
beam	In written music, the horizontal line connecting eighth notes, used in place of *flags*.
beat box	Electronic *drum machine*.
beater	The stick (with various types of head) used to hit percussion instruments.
beats	The third throbbing sound heard when two notes of slightly differing frequency are played together.
beaucoup (F)	Much.
bebend (G)	Trembling, *tremolo*.
bebop	The style of modern jazz that appeared c. 1945, and was first associated with New York musicians working around 52nd Street. Charlie Parker, Dizzy Gillespie, Bud Powell, Max Roach, Charles Mingus and Thelonious Monk were important contributors. Originally *rebop*, later called *bop*.
Bebung (G)	Trembling. Specifically, *vibrato* or *tremolo* obtained by rocking the finger.
bec (F)	Beak. The mouthpiece of a *single reed instrument*.
bécarre (F)	The *natural* sign.
Becken (G)	*Cymbals*.
bedächtig (G)	Careful, thoughtful, steady and unhurried.
Bedarfsfall (G)	'Need-case'. In case of need.
bedeutend (G)	Important.
bedrohlich (G)	Menacing.
begeistert (G)	Inspired, enthused.
begleiten (G)	To accompany, to come/go with.
beguine	Latin-American dance of Caribbean origin.
bahaglich (G)	Agreeably.
behend (G)	Nimble.
beherzt (G)	Courageous.
beide (G)	Both.
Beifall (G)	Applause.
beinahe (G)	Almost.
Beispiel (G)	Example.
Beisser (G)	Biter, i.e. *mordent*.

beklemmt, **beklommen** (G)	Oppressed.
bel	A unit for measuring the relative level of power, voltage, current or sound intensity.
bel canto (It)	Beautiful singing, beautiful song. A vocal method associated with singing of the Italian school of the seventeenth and eighteenth centuries, wherein beauty and finish of tone and delivery were considered above declamatory or dramatic effect.
belebend, belebt (G)	Animating, animated.
Beleuchtung (G)	Lighting.
Beleuchtungschef (G)	Lighting director.
Beleuchtungsmeister (G)	Lighting designer.
bell	**1.** Hollow cup-shaped resonating vessel that vibrates when struck by an internal clapper or an external hammer. **2.** The flared end of brass and woodwind instruments.
bellezza, con (It)	Beautifully, with beauty.
bellicoso (It)	Warlike. Bellicose.
bell tree	A set of small bells mounted vertically one upon the next, on a central rod.
belly	The front (upper) surface of a stringed instrument.
belustigend (G)	Amusing, fun.
bémol (F), **bemolle** (It)	*Flat*. Flat sign.
ben, bene (It)	Well, very, much.
bend (jazz)	Changing the pitch of a note.
beneplacito, **beneplacimento** (It)	'Good pleasure'. *Ad libitum*.
bequadro (It)	The *natural* sign.
bequem (G)	Comfortable.
bercement (F)	Rocking, lulling, swaying.
berceuse	*Lullaby*, cradle song.
bereite vor (G)	Make ready, prepare.
bereits (G)	Already, previously.
bergerette (F)	A shepherd's song.
berimbau (P)	Wooden bow with metal string and gourd resonator. (Brazilian.)
beruhigen (G)	To make restful.
Bes (G)	B double flat.
beschleunigen (G)	To speed up.
beseelt (G)	Animated.
Besetzung (G)	Instrumentation, cast.

bestimmt (G)	With decision, definite, decided.
betend (G)	Praying.
betont (G)	Stressed, accented.
Betrübnis (G)	Sorrow.
betrübt (G)	Saddened.
beweglich (G)	Agile.
bewegt (G)	Moved.
Bewegung (G)	Rate of motion or speed. Emotion, commotion.
bhangra	A range of popular Punjabi music.
bianca (It)	*Half note* or *minim*. Italian for 'white'.
big band	A combination of brass, saxes and rhythm, usually of between twelve and twenty musicians. The standard instrumentation is now four trumpets, four trombones, five saxophones, piano, bass, drums and sometimes guitar, though it is common to hear bands with as many as ten brass. Bands of the big band era (1938-1945) were frequently smaller than this. Benny Goodman's band, the leading swing band of the pre-war era, had only five brass and four saxophones.
Billboard	American music industry magazine.
binary form	Form where an initial section is followed by a complementary section (AB).
binaural	A stereo recording technique which places the microphones in positions equivalent to the human ears.
bis (F), (It)	Twice. Indicates the repetition of a short passage.
bis (G)	Until.
bisbigliando (It)	A whispering effect, used on the harp.
bisbigliato (It)	Whispered.
biscroma (It)	Thirty-second note, demisemiquaver.
bis zum Schluß (G)	To the end.
bit	Binary dig**IT**. The smallest piece of digital information, which can have the value of either 0 or 1.
bitonal	Simultaneous use of two keys.
bittend (G)	Entreating.
biwa	A Japanese *lute* with four strings.
bizzarro (It)	Bizarre, whimsical.
blackout	Blackout. The (sudden) extinguishing of lights in the theater.
black pudding	*Serpent.*
blackstick	*Clarinet.*

blanche (F)　Half note or minim. French for 'white'.
Blasinstrument (G)　Wind instrument.
Blasmusik (G)　Wind music.
Blech (G)　Literally 'sheet metal', i.e. brass.
Blechbläser (G)　Brass player.
Blechblasinstrument (G)　Brass instrument.
Blechinstrumente (G)　Brass instruments.
Blechmusik (G)　Brass (band) music.
bleiben (G)　To remain.
block chords　Originally a style of piano or organ playing, employing five-part harmony, in which the melody is doubled at the lower octave. Its origin is attributed to the jazz organist Milt Buckner, but the popularizer of the style was George Shearing. Glen Miller famously used an orchestrated version in which a clarinet took the melody, and a tenor saxophone doubled the melody at the lower octave.

Blockflöte (G)　Block flute. *Recorder*.
bloco,
bloco de Carnaval (P)　A group of people who parade during *Carnaval*.
bloss (G)　Mere, merely.
bluegrass　A type of country music originating in the Appalachian mountains, using violin and banjo, and sometimes mandolin, guitar and *Dobro*.
blue note　A flattened note, usually the third or seventh of the chord (or scale). On moveable pitch instruments the flattening may be approximate, at the whim of the performer. See *blues scale*.
blues　**1. Form**: A blues is usually in a repetitive cycle of twelve bar *(measure) choruses*, and in its simplest form uses only chords I, IV and V, the *primary triads*. This has sometimes been referred to as the 'three chord trick'.

A blues at its most simple would be: F/F/F/F7/B♭ B♭/F/F/C7/B♭7/F/F//. Each chord lasts for one measure.

2. Feeling: A feeling of great sadness.
blues harp　Diatonic *harmonica* (mouth organ).
blues scale　Used to epitomize or evoke the blues feeling. For example, in the key of F, it is usually, but not always, F, A♭, B♭, B, C, E♭, F.

Blumlein pair　A method of setting a pair of stereo microphones

	across each other, so that each microphone is at 45 degrees to the sound source. Named after Alan Blumlein in the 1930s.
BMI	Broadcast Music Incorporated. An American performing rights society.
bocal	The *crook* of a bassoon.
bocca chiusa (It)	Closed mouth.
bocca ridente (It)	With the mouth in a smile (singing).
boceto (Sp)	Sketch.
bodhrán	An Irish drum (like a large *tambourine* and usually without the jingles) played with a double-ended stick.
Boehm system	An arrangement of the keys and rings on woodwind instruments. It takes its name from Theobald Boehm (1793-1881), and has been applied effectively to the flute and clarinet, less so to the oboe and bassoon.
Bogen (G)	*Bow*.
bohémien, bohémienne (F)	Gypsy.
Bohrung (G)	Bore.
bois (F)	Wood.
boîte (F)	Box. The swell box of an organ.
bolero	A Spanish dance in triple time.
bomb (jazz)	A sudden and unexpected drum accent that was a feature of the *bebop* style of modern jazz.
bombard	Bass *shawm*.
bombarda (It)	*Euphonium*.
bombardon	Brass instrument of the tuba family.
bombo (P)	The largest Brazilian bass drum.
bones	A pair of sticks (or bones, or *spòons*) held together in one hand and clicked against each other.
bongos	Small one-headed drums from Cuba, usually fixed as a pair, and played with the hands.
boogie-woogie (jazz)	A solo piano jazz style popular in the 1930s and later, characterized by an insistent and powerful eighth note bass.
book	Repertoire. Refers to the book (or *pad*) of band parts.
boom	An extendable pole on which a microphone is carried.
bootleg	An illegal copy of something.
bop (bebop)	See *bebop*.

borre, borree	Old English spellings of *bourrée*.
bossa nova	A Brazilian dance and rhythm, popular from the late 1950s.
bottleneck	A tube that fits over a finger on the fretting hand of a guitarist. Used for *slide guitar* playing.
bouche fermée (F)	Closed mouth singing, humming.
bouchés, sons (F)	Stopped notes in horn playing.
bouffe (F)	Comical.
bounced	**1.** Rhythmic playing. Instruction which refers to the swung manner in which eighth notes are to be played. **2.** Moving recordings from track to track.
bourrée, borry, bore	Seventeenth century French dance, part of a *suite*.
bout (F)	End.
bouts	The curves in the ribs (sides) of a violin or guitar.
bouzouki	A Greek string instrument, fretted, with a long neck and four sets of double strings.
bow	The device drawn across the strings of an instrument to generate a sound. It is a wooden stick, of adjustable length, strung with horsehair.
bowing	The technique of the use of a *bow*.
bows	Music played while entertainers leave the stage. Also called *tabs, curtain music*, or play-off.
boyau (F)	*Catgut.*
bpm	**B**eats **p**er **m**inute.
Br.	Abbreviation for *Bratschen* (*violas*).
Brabançonne, La	The Belgian National Anthem.
braccio and gamba	Terms that distinguish the *violin* family from the *viol family*. The instruments of the viol family were held downwards, resting between the legs, hence *viole da gamba* or leg viols. Thus all upward-held instruments were named arm viols, or *viole da braccio*.
brace	Perpendicular curved line combined with a *bracket* that joins the two *staves* in piano music.
bracket	Perpendicular straight line that joins the two staves in piano music, or joins multiple staves of associated instruments in a *score*.
branle, bransle, brawl, braul	French rustic dance, from 1500 onwards.
bras (F)	Arm.
brass band	A band comprised entirely of brass instruments, plus percussion.

brass instruments, brass family — Wind instruments formerly made of metal, though may now be made from other materials, and played by buzzing the lips into a cup or funnel shaped *mouthpiece*. (Certain metal wind instruments - e.g. *saxophone, flute, sarrusophone* - are not members of the brass family.)

Bratsche (G) — *Viola.*

Brautlied (G) — Bridal song.

bravoure (F) — Bravery, gallantry.

bravura (It) — Skill, brilliance.

brawl, brawle — Old English name for *branle*.

break —
1. A between-phrases gap in a melodic line.
2. The point where the human voice changes from chest to head register.
3. An interruption of the rhythm for two or four measures, usually filled by a solo instrument.
4. Instrumental solo, usually of eight measures or more, in a predominantly vocal performance.

brega (P) — Disparaging word for cheap romantic songs.

breit (G) — Broad, expansive.

breve — A note twice the length of a whole note or semibreve. No longer used.

bridge —
1. Middle section of a popular song. Also called the *release, middle eight* or channel. In a thirty-two bar tune the bridge is normally eight measures long, but bridges of other lengths are sometimes heard.
2. The arch-shaped piece of wood that supports the strings on a string instrument.

brillante (It), **brillant** (F) — Brilliant.

brindisi (It) — Toast (drink).

brio (It) — Vigor, animation.

brisé (F) — Broken. Spread (guitar), detached (bowed strings).

broken tenth — A chord played on the piano in which the notes are not all played simultaneously, but are 'crushed' swiftly one after the other. Not all players have hands large enough to span a tenth cleanly.

broken time — Passage where the rhythm section plays intermittently, as opposed to supplying a regular pulse.

brume (F) — Mist.

Brummeisen (G) — *Jew's harp.*

Brummscheit (G) — *Tromba marina.*

bruscamente (It)	Brusquely.
brushes (jazz)	An instruction to the drummer to play with wire (sometimes plastic) brushes.
Brustwerk (G)	Choir organ.
buccolico (It)	Bucolic, rustic.
bucket (jazz)	A type of mute used by brass instruments. A short cylindrical container, which clips over the end of the bell. Sound-absorbent material inside the container quietens and modifies the tone.
buée (F)	Mist.
buffo, buffa (It)	Comic.
buffonesco (It)	Droll, buffoon-like.
bugle	A conical bore brass instrument with no valves, and hence limited to notes in the harmonic series. It is used (mainly by the military) for simple calls and for signalling.
Bühne (G)	Stage.
Bühnenarbeiter (G)	Stagehand.
Bühnenbild (G)	Set.
Bühnenbildner (G)	Designer.
Bühnenmeister (G)	Stage manager.
Bühnenmusik (G)	*Incidental music*.
bulk eraser	A device for erasing spools of magnetic recording tape swiftly without having to run them through a tape machine.
bullroarer	A thin flat blade, usually of wood, attached to a cord. By whirling the blade a whirring sound is produced. Also called *thunder stick* or *whizzer*.
burden or burthen	A recurring line of words (or nonsense sounds) after the verses of a *ballad*.
burla (It)	Jest.
burlesco, burlesca (It)	Burlesque, jocular.
burletta (It)	Comic *operetta*. Light musical entertainment in eighteenth century Britain.
business	On-stage activity, usually non-musical, adding to the dramatic effect.
busk	To play by ear, without music.
busker	Street entertainer.
button	The pin at the end of a violin which bears the pull of the strings.
BWV	Bach-Werke-Verzeichnis. A catalog of the works of J.S. Bach, compiled by Wolfgang Schmieder.
byte	In *synthesis*, eight bits of information make one byte.

C

C. A. — *Coll' Arco.*

cabaca — Latin American percussion instrument, originally a gourd (seed pod) covered with a network of threaded beads. Nowadays frequently a cylinder (fitted with a handle) with a corrugated periphery against which a band of metal rods is rubbed.

cabaletta, cabbaletta —
1. A short *aria.*
2. The final section of some arias, with motoric rhythm.

cabinet — Box in which amplification speakers are housed.

caccia (It) — Hunt, chase.

cachucha (Sp) — Type of Spanish dance.

cacophony — Loud discordant sound.

cadence — Melody or harmony towards the end of a section or phrase. Has been likened to musical punctuation marks. The various categories of cadence (e.g. *plagal, perfect, imperfect*, etc.) apply only to tonal or modal music, before the advent of *polytonality, atonality, minimalism*, etc.

cadenza (It) — Literally means 'cadence' - but now refers to the virtuoso flourish before the *cadence* in, for example, a *concerto.*

cadenzato (It) — Cadenced. Rhythmical.

caesura — A pause or break, indicated by a pair of double lines sometimes colloquially known as *tramlines.*

caisse (F) — Box, drum.

caisse claire (F) — Snare drum.

caisse grosse (F) — Bass drum.

caisse roulante (F) — Tenor drum.

caisse sourde (F) — Tenor drum.

caixa (P) — Snare drum.

caixeta (P) — *Wood block* with deep indentation or hollow. (Brazilian.)

Cajun — Folk music of the French speaking settlers of Louisiana. Deported from Nova Scotia, which the French called Acadia, they were known as Acadiens or Cajuns.

cakewalk — Nineteenth century American dance. First appeared in southern plantations. A forerunner of *ragtime.*

calando (It) — Getting softer, dying away, lowering.

calcando (It)	Trampling. Quickening gradually.
calinda, calenda	South American dance of African origin.
call and answer,	*Antiphony.*
call and response	
calliope	A set of steam whistles played by a keyboard, a steam-actuated organ.
calma (It), **calme** (F)	Calm, tranquil.
calmando, calmato (It)	Calming, calmed.
calore (It)	Heat, passion.
calypso	A type of topical narrative song, from Trinidad. Popular in Britain and USA in the 1940s and 1950s.
cambiare (It)	To change.
cambiata (It)	In counterpoint a *nota cambiata*, or *changing note*, is a nonharmonic note inserted between a *dissonance* and its *resolution*, and approached or quitted by a leap of a third.
camera (It)	Chamber, room.
camerata (It)	Club or society, in particular those in Florence at the end of the sixteenth century. Today sometimes used as the name for a chamber orchestra.
camminando (It)	Walking, proceeding, pushing on.
campana, campane (It)	Bell, bells.
campanella (It)	Little bell, *glockenspiel.*
campanetta (It)	*Glockenspiel.*
campanology	The study of bells.
Canaries, Canarie, Canary	Elizabethan dance in triple time, mentioned by Shakespeare. Believed to originate in the Canary Islands.
can-can, or **chahut**	Boisterous and allegedly shocking dance, dating from 1840, and later associated with Paris cabaret.
canción (Sp)	Song.
C&W	Country and Western.
canon	In *counterpoint,* a melody that is imitated exactly by a following voice.
canon cancrizans	See *crab canon.*
cans	Headphones.
cantabile (It)	Singable, singingly.
cantador (P)	Troubadour from northeastern and central Brazil.
cantando (It)	Singing.
cantare (It)	To sing.
cantata (It)	Sung. A sacred or secular vocal work with solos, choruses and orchestral accompaniment.

cantate (F)	*Cantata.*
cantatrice (It)	Female singer.
cante hondo (Sp)	'Deep song.' A style of Spanish flamenco song.
canti carnascialeschi (It)	Carnival songs.
canticle	A non-metrical bible hymn used in the liturgy of the Christian Church.
cantiga	Spanish or Portuguese folk song.
cantilena (It)	Melodic song.
cantilène (F)	*Cantilena.*
cantillation	Chanting in free rhythm in a *plainsong* style.
cantino (It)	The highest string. See *chanterelle.*
canto (It)	Song, melody. The highest voice.
canto fermo (It)	*Cantus firmus.*
cantor	The singer who intones the first words of *psalms*, *antiphons* and *hymns*.
cantus firmus (L)	Fixed song, melody. In an ecclesiastical chant the pre-existing melody that serves as the theme for a polyphonic piece.
canzona, canzone, canzoni (It)	A song or *ballad*. Songs.
canzonet, canzonetta (It)	Diminutive of *canzona*. A short song.
caoine	Irish funeral song, with wailing.
Capellmeister (G)	*Kapellmeister.*
capoeira (P)	Afro-Brazilian dance/martial arts form brought to Brazil by Bantu slaves from Angola.
capotasto, capo d'astro, capodastro (It), **capodastère** (F), **Capodaster** (G)	The nut at the top of the fingerboard of an instrument, over which the strings pass. A movable capotasto is frequently seen being used by guitarists, to facilitate playing in remote keys.
cappella (It)	Chapel.
capriccio (It), **caprice** (F)	Instrumental music played in a free style.
capriccioso (It)	Capricious.
caressant (F)	Caressing.
carezzando, carezzevole (It)	Caressing, caressingly.
carillon	A set of bells played from a keyboard.
carioca (P)	Someone or something from the city of Rio de Janeiro.
Carnaval (P)	Four days of celebration before Ash Wednesday. Shrove Tuesday. See *Mardi Gras.*
carol	A Christmas song.
carrée (F)	Square. The *breve.*

cassa (It)	Box. Large drum.
cassa grande,	Bass drum.
gran cassa (It)	
cassa rullante (It)	Tenor drum.
cassation	Type of eighteenth century ensemble composition in several movements.
cassette	Small cartridge containing magnetic tape.
castagnette (It),	*Castanets. Kastagnetten.*
castagnettes (F)	
castanets	Spanish percussion instrument consisting of two spoon-shaped pieces of wood, hinged at the base by string, and rhythmically clicked together by the fingers.
castrato	A (castrated) adult male singer with an alto or soprano voice. A eunuch.
catalán (Sp), **catalane** (F)	A Spanish dance from Catalonia.
catch	A humorous, sometimes bawdy, composition for three or four voices, structured similarly to a *round.*
catgut	Cord made from the intestines of sheep and other animals, used for making strings for the violin and guitar family.
cavaquinho (P)	A small plucked *lute* of Portugal and Brazil, between a *guitar* and a *mandolin.*
cavatina	A short simple song without repeats. Also used for a songlike instrumental piece.
caxixi (P)	Small wicker container, filled with seeds, used as a shaker in *capoeira.*
CD	Compact Disc.
cebell	Type of *gavotte*, English in origin, and faster in style.
cédez (F)	Give way.
céilidh	Night-long informal Scottish social gathering, mainly for song and instrumental music.
celere (It)	Quick, speedy.
celesta, céleste	A percussion instrument, with steel bars struck by hammers operated from a keyboard.
céleste	On some pianos, a pedal that inserts a soft cloth between the hammer and the strings.
cello	Abbreviation of *violoncello.*
cembalo	*Harpsichord.* Italian for *dulcimer.*
cent	Unit of pitch equal to one hundredth of a semitone.
cercar la nota (It)	An anticipation of the next note.

cervelas (F)	'Sausage'. (Saveloy). *Racket.*
Ces (G)	C flat.
Ceses (G)	C double flat.
cetera, cetra (It)	*Cittern.*
cha-cha, cha-cha-cha	Latin American dance.
chaconne (F)	A piece built on a series of variations on a bass line or a harmonic progression. Based on a Spanish dance in triple meter, it is usually a slow instrumental piece. See *passacaglia.*
chacony	Old English for *chaconne.*
chahut	See *can-can.*
chaleur (F)	Warmth.
chalumeau	The low register of the *clarinet*, from (written) bottom E to throat B♭. Named after an early single reed instrument which used only this register.
chamber music	Art music for a small ensemble.
chamber orchestra	Small orchestra.
champêtre (F)	Rural, rustic.
chance music	See *aleatoric.*
change ringing	A bell-ringing pattern so that the sequence of bells changes with each repetition.
changes	**1.** The outlines of the patterns used by bell-ringers in change ringing. **2.** Short for 'chord changes', frequently and incorrrectly referred to as 'chord sequence' rather than 'chord progression'. See *sequence.*
changez (F)	Change.
changgo, changko	Two-headed Korean drum.
changing note	See *cambiata.*
channel	Electronic pathway.
chanson (F)	Song.
chanson sans paroles (F)	Song without words.
chant	**1.** Unaccompanied sacred vocal music, usually *monophonic.* **2.** To sing.
chantant (F)	Singing.
chanter (F)	To sing.
chanter	The pipe of a bagpipe on which the melody is played. For practice purposes it is detached from the air bag and blown directly with the lips.
chanterelle (F)	The highest string on any stringed instrument. The E string on the violin.
chaque (F)	Each, every.

characteristic piece, **character piece** **Charakterstück** (G)	Short instrumental piece built upon one mood or idea.
charivari (F)	*Characteristic piece.* Rough extemporized music performed outdoors on kitchen utensils, before the abode of an individual of whom the community wishes to make fun or deride. Sometimes used as a mock *serenade* for newlyweds.
charleston	A dance popular in the 1920s.
chart(s)	**1.** Instrumental score for a jazz or pop ensemble. **2.** Popularity lists of recordings, rated by sales.
chase, chase chorus	Two jazz soloists alternating in eight measure or four measure sections (*eights* or *fours*), in a spirit of competition.
chasse, cor de (F)	Hunting horn.
che (It)	Who, which.
chef d'attaque (F)	Leader, concertmaster.
chest voice	The lower register of the voice.
chevalet (F)	*Bridge* (of string instruments). Literally 'trestle'.
cheville (F)	*Peg.*
chiaro, chiara, **chiaramente, chiarezza** (It)	Clear, distinct, clearly, clarity.
chiasso (It)	See *charivari.*
chiave (It)	*Clef.*
chica (Sp)	Earlier form of the *fandango.*
Chicago jazz	A type of jazz that emerged in Chicago during the 1920s, a sort of developed (white) New Orleans Jazz or *Dixieland*, and using larger instrumentation than hitherto, often including the tenor saxophone. Leading practitioners were Bix Beiderbecke, Eddie Condon, Bud Freeman, Benny Goodman, Jimmy McPartland and Dave Tough. See *Second Chicago School.*
chiesa (It)	Church.
chifonie (F)	Early name for the *hurdy-gurdy.*
chimes	Set of tuned metal tubes.
Chinese pavilion	See *jingling Johnny.*
Chinese temple blocks	Skull-shaped hollow blocks of wood, tuned approximately to a *pentatonic* scale and thus in several sizes. Used as part of a *swing era* dance band drummer's kit, and played with sticks, mallets or beaters. Similar to *Korean temple blocks.*

Chinese wood block	Rectangular block of partially hollowed hardwood, emitting a harsh sound when hit with a drumstick. Part of a jazz drum kit. Other names are *clog box* and *tap box*.
chitarra (It)	*Guitar.*
chitarrone, chittarone	A *lute*, a longer version of the *theorbo*.
chiuso, chiusa (It)	Closed.
chocalho (P)	Metal or wooden shaker in the shape of two cones joined at the base. Also *xocalho*.
choeur (F)	*Chorus, choir.*
choir	1. Group of singers. 2. Part of a cathedral where the choir is placed. In a church (as opposed to a cathedral) this is called the chancel.
choke cymbals	See *hi-hat*.
chops	A player's technique, or playing fitness. Jazz slang, now enjoying wider use, not restricted to wind instruments. Guitarists or drummers may be discussed in terms of their chops. Also *embouchure*.
Chor (G)	1. *Choir.* 2. *Chorus.*
choral	Pertaining to choirs and choral music.
chorale	German Lutheran hymn tune.
chorale prelude	Organ music based on a hymn.
Choral Vorspiel (G)	*Chorale prelude.*
chord	Two or more notes sounded simultaneously.
chord changes, **chord progression**	The pattern of harmonic changes onto which a melody or piece is built. Frequently, and incorrectly, referred to as a chord *sequence*.
chord symbols	System of harmonic shorthand (e.g. G7, Cm7♭5, etc.), widely used in jazz, theater and popular music. Twentieth century, originally used for fretted instruments.
chorister	Singer in a choir.
Chorleiter (G)	Choirmaster.
Chormässige **Stimmung** (G)	Choir pitch.
chôro(s) (P)	Brazilian street music for instrumental ensemble; also a musical genre developed by Heitor Villa Lobos.
Chorsänger (G)	Chorus or choir member.
Chorstimmung (G)	Choir pitch.

chorus	**1.** A group of singers of secular music, or the music sung by such a group.
	2. The refrain of a song.
	3. Electronic processing that simulates the sound of multiple instruments playing simultaneously.
chromatic	Intervals or notes outside the *diatonic* scale. Moving by half steps or semitones.
chromatique (F)	*Chromatic.*
ciaccona (It)	*Chaconne.*
cigány (Hungarian)	Gypsy.
cimbal, cimbalom,	*Dulcimer.* Metal strings mounted on a
cimbalon, cimbelom	sounding box. The strings are struck with mallets.
cimbasso (It)	Valve trombone.
cinelli (It)	*Cymbals.*
cinema organ	An electric organ installed in a cinema, for entertainment between films. Because cinema performances ran continuously, critics of the instrument held that it was used to empty the auditorium, to make room for more customers! *Theater organ.*
cinq (F)	Five, (*cinquième*, fifth).
cinque (It)	Five.
cinquième position (F)	Fifth position.
cioè (It)	That is, i.e.
cipher, ciphering	An organ note that is 'stuck' and continues to sound.
ciranda (P)	Portuguese children's circle dance.
circle of fifths	A harmonic pattern where chords resolve downwards in root movements of perfect fifths. These could be chains of dominant sevenths (e.g.G7/C7/F7/B♭7) or diatonic progressions (e.g. Am7/Dm7/G7/C) . Also known as cycle of fifths.
circular breathing	Maintaining a steady and uninterrupted stream of air in wind playing by inhaling through the nose while exhaling through the mouth. The cheeks are used as bellows.
Cis (G)	C sharp.
Cisis (G)	C double sharp.
cither	*Cittern.*
cittern	Ancient flat-backed *lute.*
civetteria (It)	Coquetry, flirtatiousness.
clairon (F)	*Bugle.*
clam	Wrong note, mistake.

clapper	The striker in the center of a *bell*.
claquebois (F)	*Xylophone.*
clarinet	Parallel bore single reed woodwind instrument, overblowing a twelfth.
clarino	Name for high trumpet playing of the seventeenth and eighteenth centuries.
clarionet	Obsolete name for *clarinet*.
clàrsach	Small ancient Celtic harp, revived in the twentieth century for folk song accompaniment.
classical, classic	Vague term, used: **1.** To distinguish serious or art music from popular, folk or jazz. **2.** To distinguish the classical period from the romantic period. **3.** As an adjective meaning time-honored or popular vintage mainstream, in phrases such as 'classic jazz', 'classic rock'.
clave, clavé	Cuban percussion instrument consisting of two cylindrical hardwood sticks (about 15-18 cms long) which are beaten together.
clavecin (F)	*Harpsichord.*
clavicembalo (It)	*Harpsichord.*
clavichord	Early keyboard instrument.
clavier	A keyboard, whether for hands or feet.
Clavierübung (G)	Clavier exercise. Title of a work by J.S.Bach.
clavioline	An early electronic keyboard instrument, with a small range and knee-controlled volume, intended to be used to supplement the piano in small dance bands. Mid-twentieth century, now obsolete.
clawhammer	Banjo picking style using the thumb and two fingers.
clef	The sign at the beginning of a piece of music that fixes the location of the notes on the *staff*.
click track	Pre-recorded metronome clicks which are played back to musicians through headphones, as guidance.
cloches (F)	Bells (orchestral).
clochette (F)	Small bell.
clog box	Percussion instrument. Small rectangular hollow wooden box, played with sticks.
close	*Cadence.*
close harmony	Harmony wherein the notes are placed as close together as possible.

clusters	Groups of notes a semitone apart, sounded simultaneously.
C-melody	A type of high tenor *saxophone* pitched in C, a tone higher than the normal B♭ tenor saxophone. Introduced to avoid the problems of *transposing*, but loved for its own qualities.
coach horn	A straight valveless brass instrument with a conical bore and bell. Originally used on stagecoaches to announce arrivals and departures, and thus also known as a *post horn*.
cobla (Catalan)	Small *wind band* which accompanies the Catalonian national dance, the *sardana*.
coda (It)	Tail. A passage at the end of a composition added to create a sense of finality.
codetta (It)	Small *coda*.
cogli, coi (It)	With the (plural).
col, coll', colla, colle (It)	With the.
colascione	Type of three-stringed *lute*, encountered in southern Europe and Germany.
colinda	A type of Romanian Christmas song.
colla parte (It)	Keep with the soloist, a direction to an accompanist.
colla punta dell' arco (It)	With the point of the bow.
coll' arco (It)	With the *bow*.
colla voce (It)	Keep with the singer, a direction to an accompanist.
collective improvisation	Simultaneous improvisation, a feature of New Orleans Jazz, and occasionally heard in other styles.
collegium musicum (L)	Musical society.
col legno (It)	With the wood. An instruction to string players to play with the back of the bow.
coll' ottava (It)	With the *octave*. A direction to a keyboard player to double notes an octave higher - or lower if *bassa* is added.
colofonia (It)	Colophony, or bow resin. *Kolophon*.
coloratura (It)	'Colored'. Refers to the decoration of a vocal melody. A *coloratura soprano* is one with a light, flexible voice.
colpo (It)	Stroke.
combo	A small band ('combination'), usually between five and ten players. Term mostly used in a jazz context.

come (It), **comme** (F)	As, similar to, like.
come down, **coming down**	When the curtain comes down. The time of the end of a performance in the theater.
come prima (It)	As before.
come sopra (It)	As above.
comic opera	A light-hearted opera.
comique (F)	Comic.
comma	1. A very small interval.
	2. Breath mark.
commedia dell' arte (It)	'Comedy of the profession'. Sixteenth century Italian parodic entertainment that influenced comic opera.
commercial music	Music that is intended primarily to make money.
commère (F)	The feminine of *compère*.
common chord	A *triad* composed of root, third and fifth.
common time	Four-four time.
common tone	A note (tone) that remains constant between two successive chords.
comodo (It)	Convenient. Comfortable.
comp, comping	To accompany, in the sense of providing an accompanying harmonic framework or bed, over which a jazz soloist will improvise. Thus, only keyboard players or guitarists will 'comp'.
compact disc	A digital form of sound recording, where a rotating disc is read by a laser (CD).
compass	The range of an instrument or voice.
compère (F)	An announcer, usually in light entertainment.
compiacevole (It)	Pleasing.
compline	Completion. The eighth and final of the daily services of the Roman Catholic Church.
composé (F)	Composed. Compound.
compound interval	Any interval greater than an octave.
compound meter, **compound time**	A time signature where the pulse (i.e. upper number) is divisible by three, e.g. 6/8, 9/8, 12/8.
compression	An electronic limitation of the dynamic range of a reproduced sound.
compressor	The electronic device that performs *compression*.
compter (F)	To count.
con (It)	With.
con amore (It)	With love.
con anima (It)	With spirit, with soul.
con brio (It)	With animation, with vigor.

concertante	A piece for two or more instruments, with orchestral accompaniment.
concert band	Large wind ensemble, also known as a *wind band*, *marching band* or *military band*.
concert grand	The largest grand piano.
concertina	A small *accordion* in the shape of a hexagonal cylinder, with buttons instead of a keyboard.
concertino	1. A short and lighter type of *concerto*.
	2. The group of soloists in a *concerto grosso*.
concert master	Leader. First violin.
concerto	A piece for soloist and large ensemble.
concerto grosso	A Baroque instrumental piece that contrasts a small ensemble (*concertino*) and a large ensemble (*ripieno*).
concert overture	A one movement orchestral work composed for the concert hall.
concert pitch	1. The pitch of a non-transposing instrument.
	2. International standard of pitch, A 440 or A 442.
concertstück	Concert piece.
concitato (It)	'Excited'. A compositional style defined and used by Monteverdi to represent emotional excitement.
concord	Without *dissonance*, harmonious, pleasant, *consonance*.
con fuoco (It)	With fire.
conga	Cuban line dance.
congada (P)	*Congo.*
conga drum	A tall (waist high) single-headed Afro-Cuban drum, played with the hands.
congo	Double-headed drum associated with the West Indies.
conjunct motion	Notes that move by step.
consecutives	Parallel intervals, a pair of notes that move so that they maintain the same interval between them.
consequent	The second phrase in a musical *period*. In a *fugue*, the *answer*.
conservatorio (It), **conservatoire** (F)	*Conservatory.*
conservatory	School of music.
conserver (F)	To preserve. Used in the sense of 'to preserve the rhythm'.
console	On an organ, the place where the player sits.
consonance, consonant	In harmony, pleasant, without *discord*.
con sordino (It)	With mute.

consort	A *Renaissance* chamber ensemble.
conte (F)	Tale, story.
continuo	*Basso continuo.*
contrabass,	**1.** Double bass.
contrabasso (It)	**2.** Prefix to describe any very low pitched member of an instrumental family, e.g. contrabass clarinet, contrabass saxophone.
contractor	Person responsible for hiring professional musicians for casual engagements. *Fixer.*
contradanza (It)	Country dance.
contralto	The lowest female voice.
contrapuntal	Use of *counterpoint.*
contrary motion	Two voices moving simultaneously in opposite directions.
contrebasse (F)	Double bass.
contredanse (F)	Country dance.
cool	Term used to describe a style of 1950s jazz, modelled on a 1948 Miles Davis recording, *Birth of the Cool.* Early twenty-first century slang for stylish, fashionable.
coperto (It)	Covered, muffled.
copla (Sp)	A Spanish popular song and poem in short verses.
Coppel (G)	Coupler (organ).
coprifuoco, coprifoco (It)	Curfew. Sometimes used as an evocative title for music with a bell effect.
copyist	The copyist extracts the individual parts from a composer's score and writes out playing parts. Once, copyists provided the only copies of music in circulation. Even after the widespread availability of cheap commercial printing, copyists were still essential in Hollywood, on Broadway and in other places where new music was performed. After the computer arrived, copyists used appropriate software to prepare performance parts.
copyright	The (sole) right to produce or reproduce in any material form an original literary, dramatic or musical work.
cor anglais (F)	*English horn.*
corant, coranto	See *courante.*
corda, corde (It)	String, strings.
corde (F)	String.
corde à jour,	Open string.
corde à vide (F)	

cor de basset (F)	*Basset horn.*
cor de chasse (F)	Natural hunting horn, in E♭ or D.
cor des Alpes (F)	*Alphorn.*
cor d'harmonie (F)	*French horn.*
corea (Sp)	A dance accompanied by a song.
cornemuse (F)	A type of *bagpipe* from France, blown by mouth as opposed to air provided by bellows.
cornet,	Cornet. B♭ brass instrument with three valves.
cornet à pistons (F)	
cornett, cornetto (It)	A curved instrument made of ivory or of wood enwrapped with leather, with holes covered by the player's fingers, and a cup-shaped mouthpiece.
corno (It)	Horn.
corno alto,	Names for horn players who specialized in either
corno basso (It)	the higher parts (*alto*) or lower parts (*basso*).
corno a mano (It)	Hand horn.
corno cromatico (It)	Valve horn.
corno da caccia (It)	Hunting horn.
corno di bassetto (It)	*Basset horn.*
corno inglese (It)	*English horn.*
corno ventile (It)	Valve horn.
coro (It)	*Choir, chorus.*
corps de rechange (F)	*Crook* of a brass instrument.
cor simple (F)	Natural horn.
cortège (F)	Procession.
corto, corta,	Short. Shortly.
cortamente (It)	
cotillon (F)	A lively French dance, similar to the *quadrille.*
couched harp	Old name for the *spinet.*
coulamment (F)	Flowing.
coulisse (F)	The *slide* of a *trombone* or *slide trumpet.*
counter-exposition	In a *fugue*, a second *exposition.*
counterpoint	The combination of two or more melodic lines. The interest is linear rather than vertical or chordal.
countertenor	The highest male voice.
country, country and western	Simple American popular song, late twentieth century.
coup d'archet (F)	Bowstroke.
coupler	The mechanism on a harpsichord or organ that enables the performer to connect two or more manuals or pedals or to double at an octave.
coupure (F)	Cut. Omit a portion.

courante, corrente, coranto, corant	Literally 'running', used as a movement of the *suite*.
courroie (F)	Strap.
couvert, couverte (F)	Covered.
cover, cover version	A new version (by a rival artist) of a previous hit song, often very similar to the original.
cowbell	A simple metal bell (usually of sheet metal, riveted or welded), originally fitted with a clapper and hung around the neck of a cow. A form exists without the clapper, intended to be struck by a drumstick.
cozinha (P)	Ensemble of drums, bass and assorted percussion. A rhythmic mix.
crab canon	*Canon cancrizans*. (L: crablike.) A contrapuntal piece in which one part is identical to another, but backwards.
Cracovienne, Krakowiak	Polish dance (from Cracow), a simple *polonaise*.
cradle song	See *berceuse*.
crash cymbal, Chinese crash cymbal	A large cymbal, part of a dance band or jazz kit. The Chinese version may have upturned edges, and loose rivets fitted (for sizzle).
crécelle (F)	Rattle.
Credo (L)	'I believe'. The Creed. In the *Mass*, the third part of the *Ordinary*.
crembalum (L)	*Jew's harp*.
Creole	Native, of mixed ancestry, applied to the French or Spanish people in Louisiana, USA. The famous New Orleans musicians Sidney Bechet and Jelly Roll Morton were Creole.
crescendo, cresc., cres. (It)	Increasing. Gradually becoming louder. A term frequently misused to mean louder. It is a process, not a condition. See *hairpin*.
croche (F)	Hook. Meaning an eighth note or quaver, not a *crotchet* or quarter note. (*Noire* is the French for quarter note.)
croiser, croiser les mains (F)	To cross, cross hands.
croma (It)	Eighth note, quaver.
cromatico, cromatica (It)	*Chromatic*.
crook	Curved piece of tubing fitted into a brass instrument to change its pitch.
crooning	A type of soft popular singing, introduced with the

advent of radio in the USA in the late 1920s. Banned in Italy in 1935.

cross fingering Complex fingering patterns used in woodwind playing to achieve good *intonation*, or to play chromatic notes where 'conventional' keyed fingerings are awkward or slow.

crossover Music that crosses over from one specialized area to another.

cross rhythm Different rhythm patterns played simultaneously.

crotales, crotola Tuned cymbals.

crotchet British term for quarter note.

crotchet jazz British term for jazz played in the swing style, using a bass line that plays quarter notes (crotchets).

crumhorn *Krummhorn.*

crwth Ancient plucked and bowed stringed instrument from Wales. Shaped like a *lyre* but played with a bow. An ancestor of the *violin* family. Other names are crowd, crot, cruit, chorus, *rote* and *rotta.*

csárdás *Czardas.*

cuckoo A small whistle that produces two notes in imitation of the song of the cuckoo. Used in the *Toy Symphony,* etc.

cue 1. An indication for a performer to make an entry. It may be a conductor's gesture, a spoken word, or another performer's action.
2. Small notes giving another performer's part.
3. Music placement in a film.

cuíca (P) A small Brazilian *friction drum* with a thin stick attached to the skin. A moistened cloth is used to rub the stick, and pressure is applied to the skin to produce squeaks, grunts and groans.

cuivre (F) Copper, brass. Thus the brass of the orchestra.

cuivré (F) Coppery, brassy.

cup Type of *mute* for brass instruments.

cupo (It) Dark, somber.

curtain music, curtain tune Piece played when the curtain is lowered at the end of an act or performance, beneath applause or for performers to take their bows. See *tabs.* In Japanese, ka-a-ten-my-u-jikku.

cushion dance An old dance in which a partner was chosen by dropping a cushion in front of him or her.

cut 1. To record a song.

cut, cutting contest (jazz)

cut time,
cut common time

cyclic form,
cyclical form

Cyklus (G)
cylinder (Eng),
cylindre (F),
cilindro (It)

cymbalom, cymbalon
cymbals

cymbalum orale (L)
cymbasso
czardas, csárdás,
tchardache
czimbal, czimbalom,
czimbalon

2. A track on an LP or CD.
A form of *jam session* where the aim is to outplay your fellow musicians by being more creative, and having more endurance or more virtuosity.
2/2 meter.

1. Any work in several movements.
2. A work in which the movements are connected by common musical material.
See *Zyklus*.
Rotary valve, as used in Britain and USA for the *French horn*, but used for all valved brass instruments in many countries of Europe.
Dulcimer, popular in Hungary.
Percussion instruments, being circular brass plates which can be clashed together, or played with sticks, brushes, beaters, mallets or hands. See *hi-hat*.
Jew's harp.
Verdi's name for the *tuba*.
A national dance of Hungary. *Tcharda* means tavern.
See *cymbalom*.

D

D	Abbreviation for 'Deutsch' in numbering the works of Franz Schubert, after Otto Erich Deutsch (1883-1967), scholar and editor.
d' (F)	Of, from, an abbreviation of *de*.
da (It)	Of, from.
da capo (It)	From the head, i.e. return to the beginning. Often abbreviated to *D.C.* Sometimes the words *al fine* are added, meaning then go to the point marked *fine*, the end. Alternatively, the words *al coda* can be added, meaning 'then go to the coda', which finishes the piece.
dactyl, dactylic	In poetry, the rhythm of an accented syllable plus two unaccented syllables. The science of versification is called *prosody*.
dal segno (It)	From the sign, i.e. return to the sign. Thence one plays until the word *fine* is reached, or to a double bar with a pause above it. Sometimes abbreviated to *D.S.*
damp	On a string instrument, to press on the strings to stop them sounding.
damper pedal	The piano pedal that lifts the dampers from the strings. The pedal on the right.
dampers	The part of the piano mechanism that presses on the strings until raised by the *damper pedal*.
Dämpfer (G)	*Mute.*
dance band	Any ensemble that provides music for dancing. Specifically a mid-twentieth century small wind band with *rhythm section* and (usually) a singer, playing commercial pop music of the period.
danse (F), **danza** (It)	Dance.
danzon, danzonetta	Dances of the *rumba* family.
Dargason	An English country dance tune, used in St. Paul's Suite (Holst).
Darstellung (G)	Representation, presentation.
darunter (G)	Thereunder.
dasselbe (G)	The same.
DAT	**D**igital **A**udio **T**ape.
Dauer (G)	Duration.
dauernd (G)	Enduring, lasting.
Daumen (G)	Thumb.

dazu (G)	Thereto. In addition.
dB	Decibel.
D.C.	*Da Capo*.
de, d' (F)	Of, from.
dead	Adjective to describe an acoustic with a short reverberation time.
débile (F), **debole** (It)	Weak.
début (F)	Beginning, opening, first public appearance.
decay	The dying away of a note or sound.
déchant (F)	*Descant.*
decibel	Unit of loudness (intensity) but also used for measuring power, voltage and current.
décidé (F)	Decided, with decision.
decimette	A piece for ten performers.
deciso (It)	Decided.
deck	Record turntable.
decken (G)	To cover.
declamando, declamato (It)	In a declamatory style.
découpler (F)	To uncouple.
decrescendo, decresc., decres. (It)	Decreasing, decreased. *Diminuendo*.
decresciuto (It)	Decreased.
défaut (F)	Fault or lack.
degaussing	Demagnetizing.
degree	A note of the scale, referred to by number, e.g. 'first degree', 'second degree', etc.
dehors (F)	Outside. Prominently.
deklamieren (G)	To declame.
de la (F)	Of the, from the.
delay	In *synthesis* or *sound reinforcement*, an electronic device for slowing the signal and thus producing an echo effect.
delicato (It)	Delicate.
délié (F)	Untied.
delirio (It)	Frenzy.
delizioso (It)	Delicious, sweet.
démancher (F)	*Manche* is the neck of a stringed instrument. *Démancher,* (to 'un-neck'), means to move the hand away from the neck and nearer to the *bridge*.
demi (F)	Half.
demi-jeu (F)	To play at half power. Literally 'half-play'.
demi-pause (F)	Half-rest. A half note (*minim*) rest.

demisemiquaver	Thirty-second note.
demi-ton (F)	*Semitone.*
demi-voix (F)	Half voice. Half power.
demo	Demonstration recording.
demütig, demüthig (G)	Meek.
dennoch (G)	Nevertheless.
der, die, das,	The.
dem, den (G)	
derb (G)	Firm, solid, rough.
derby	A derby hat is a bowler hat. A muting effect (with little tone coloration) was originally obtained by brass players placing a derby hat over the bells of their instruments. Later a metal or fiber mute in the shape of a hat was marketed.
derselbe (G)	The same.
des (F)	Of the.
des (G)	Of the.
Des (G)	D flat.
desafio (P)	Poetic improvisational contests between two vocalists.
descant	Melody or counterpoint sung above the main song, or the upper voice in part-music.
Deses (G)	D double flat.
desiderio (It)	Desire, longing.
desinvolto,	Ease.
desinvoltura (It)	
desk	Mixing console in a recording studio.
dessous (F)	Below, under.
dessus (F)	Above, over.
desto (It)	Wide-awake.
destro, destra (It)	Right. (Can also mean dextrous.)
de suite (F)	One following the other. Immediately.
détaché (F)	Detached.
determinato (It)	Determined.
detune	To deliberately tune sound sources a few *cents* differently, to produce *beats*.
deutlich (G)	Distinct, clearly.
Deutsch (G)	German.
deux (F)	Two.
deuxième (F)	Second.
deux temps (F)	In 2/2 time.
development	The elaboration of musical material.
devoto (It)	Devout, with devotion.

devozione (It)	Devotion.
Dezime (G)	Tenth. (Interval.)
di (It)	By, from, of.
Diabolus in musica (L)	The Devil in music. The medieval name for the *tritone*.
diapason	1. The basic tone of the organ.
	2. The *range* or *compass* of a voice or instrument.
	3. Bass strings of the *Renaissance lute*.
diapente (Greek)	Perfect fifth interval.
diaphragm	The flexible partition of muscle and tendons separating the upper part of the body from the lower. Much referred to in the teaching of singing and wind playing.
diatonic	Notes within a major or minor key.
Dichtung (G)	Poem.
dick (G)	Thick.
didjeridu, didgeridoo	Australian aboriginal wind instrument (trumpet) made from the branch of a tree, about 1.8 meters long. The playing technique involves *circular breathing*.
dieci (It)	Ten.
dièse (F), **diesis** (It)	Sharp. Half-step.
Dies Irae (L)	Day of Wrath. A section of the *Requiem Mass*, wherein the *plainsong* tune of the *Dies Irae* is quoted.
digital	The numerical representation of data, done electronically.
digital piano	An electronic piano using *digital* sampling to create the sound.
diluendo (It)	Fading.
dilungando (It)	Lengthening.
diminished interval	A minor or *perfect interval* lowered by a half-step.
diminished scale	A regular scale made up of the steps: tone, semitone, tone, semitone, etc. The eight notes could also be generated by superimposing two *diminished seventh* chords, hence the name.
diminished seventh	A chord made up of root, minor third, diminished fifth and diminished seventh, that is, three minor thirds. It occurs on the raised seventh degree of a minor scale, e.g. B, D, F, A♭ in the key of C minor.
diminuendo, dimin., dim. (It)	Gradually becoming softer. See *hairpin*.
diminution	Shortening the duration of note values in a melody or theme.

di molto (It)	Of much.
DIN	Deutsche Industrie Normale. German industry body overseeing technical standardization. This abbreviation is most frequently encountered in descriptions of connector types.
di nuovo (It)	Anew.
dip (jazz)	A brief lowering of pitch.
direct to disk	1. Recording direct to a master, without first using tape. (Obsolete.) 2. Recording straight to a hard disk, for later replay or editing.
dirge	Originally, a piece played at a funeral or memorial service. Later used to describe any slow and somber piece.
Dirigent, Leiter (G)	Conductor.
Dirigentenpult (G)	Rostrum.
Dirigentenstab (G)	Conductor's *baton*.
dirigieren (G)	To conduct.
Dis (G)	D sharp.
disc	General term covering several types of domestic sound reproduction, including the 78 rpm shellac disc, 33 rpm vinyl disc (LP), Compact Disc (CD), MiniDisc (MD) and Digital Video/Versatile Disc (DVD).
disco, discotheque	A dance club where records are played. These clubs led to the rise of a distinct style of disco music, and to *DJs*, *scratching*, *hip-hop*, *drum and bass*, *garage*, etc.
discord	Unpleasant or dissonant sounds. The opposite of *concord*.
discreto (It)	Discreet, reserved.
discrezione, discretezza (It)	Discretion, reserve.
disinvolto (It)	Self-possessed. Easy-going.
Disis (G)	D double sharp.
disjunct	Moving by intervals larger than a *second*.
disk, diskette	Magnetic computer disc, as opposed to the spelling *disc,* which is used for *AV* media.
Diskant (G)	*Descant.*
disperato (It)	Desperate.
dissonance, dissonant	*Discord.*
distanza (It)	Distance.
distinto (It)	Distinct, clear.

distortion	An effect that alters the purity of a sound. Usually refers to electronic alteration, but this is frequently imitative of techniques (e.g. *fuzz tone, growl, wah-wah*) used in playing traditional instruments.
dithyramb (Eng), **dithyrambe** (F), **ditirambo** (It)	Ancient Greek choral hymn, wild in nature.
diva (It)	'Divine woman'. 'Goddess'. Term (of adulation) for a female singer, usually for an operatic soprano.
diversions	A synonym for *variations*.
divertimento (It)	An amusement. A lighter work, usually for a small ensemble.
divertissement (F)	A dance or ballet included in an opera or play to add variety.
divisi, div. (It), **divisés** (F)	Divided. A direction to orchestral players that the music is divided into separate parts, and they are no longer playing in *unison*.
divisions	Obsolete term for *variations*. Originally, in the seventeenth and eighteenth centuries, the splitting up of the notes of a tune into shorter notes, to create a variation.
divoto, divotamente (It)	Devout, devoutly, devotedly.
dix (F)	Ten.
Dixieland (jazz)	Early jazz, or jazz played in that style. The name is said to come from the ten dollar bill in Louisiana having the French for ten (*dix*) printed on it.
DJ	**D**isc **J**ockey. Person who plays records, and *scratches*.
do, doh	The first note of the *diatonic* scale.
Dobro	Commercial name for an early twentieth century guitar with a circular metal *resonator* on the belly. Developed by the **Do**pyera **Bro**thers in the USA.
doch (G)	However, yet.
dodecaphonic	*Twelve-note* music.
doglia (It)	Sorrow.
doigt (F)	Finger.
doit, doivent (F)	Must.
doit, doink	A jazz effect where the note (usually on a wind instrument, especially trumpet) is sounded and then glissed upwards, fading onto an indeterminate pitch.
Dolby	An electronic device, patented in 1969 by Ray

Dolby, that reduces unwanted noise on a recording.

dolce (It)	Sweet, soft.
dolente (It)	Doleful, sad, mournful.
dolore (It)	Dolor, pain, grief.
Dolzflöte (G)	Soft flute-toned organ stop.
Dom (G)	Cathedral.
dominant	The fifth degree of the diatonic major or minor scale.
dominant seventh	Seventh chord built on the *dominant*, e.g. G,B,D,F in the key of C major or minor. See *secondary dominant*.
domra	A type of *balalaika*.
dongle	A small copyright protection device (piece of hardware) that is needed to complete a circuit.
Donner (G)	Thunder.
dopo (It)	After.
doppel (G)	Double.
Doppel B, Doppel-be (G)	*Double flat.*
Doppelchor (G)	Double chorus.
Doppelfagott (G)	Double bassoon.
Doppelfuge (G)	Double fugue.
Doppelganznote (G)	Double whole note. *Breve.*
Doppelgriff (G)	*Double stop.*
Doppelkreuz (G)	*Double sharp.*
doppeln (G)	To double.
Doppelschlag (G)	'Double stroke'. *Turn.*
Doppeltaktnote (G)	Double-measure note. Two measure note. A double whole note, or *breve*.
doppelt so schnell (G)	Double as fast.
doppio (It)	Double.
doppio movimento (It)	Double speed, twice as fast.
Doppler effect	An effect heard when the source of a sound is moved relative to the listener - the 'approaching and passing fire engine' effect. The change in distance between source and listener alters the pitch. Named after the Austrian physicist C. J. Doppler (1803-1853).
Dorian mode	A *mode* whose step-pattern is the same as playing D to D in the key of C major.
dot, dotted note	A dot written after a note increases its value by one half. Written above or below the note it is an instruction to play *staccato*.

double (F)	Old term for *variation*.
doublé (F)	The *turn* (musical ornament).
double	**1.** To play more than one instrument.
	2. To play the same part.
double bar	Double perpendicular lines at the end of a section of music, or at the end of a composition. A double bar does not necessarily coincide with a bar line - it has no rhythmic function.
double bass	The lowest pitched member of the violin family. The four strings are normally tuned E, A, D, G.
double bémol (F)	*Double flat.*
double concerto	A *concerto* with two solo instruments.
double croche (F)	Sixteenth note or semiquaver. Literally 'double hook.'
double-density (jazz)	A woodwind (mostly *saxophone*) cross fingering technique whereby different tone colors (densities) can be obtained for the same note.
double dièse (F)	*Double sharp.*
double dot	A notational device invented by Leopold Mozart. Two dots increase the length of a note by three-quarters of its original duration.
double flat	Written in front of a note, lowering the pitch of that note by one whole tone.
double reed	The paired reeds which are the sound source of the instruments of the *oboe* and *bassoon* families. See also *Heckelphone*, *sarrusophone*, *tenoroon*.
double sharp	Cross sign, placed before a note, raising the pitch of that note by one whole tone.
double stem	A note that is stemmed both up and down, indicating that two parts share that pitch.
double stop, **double stopping**	Stopping two strings simultaneously.
double time	Twice as fast as before. Sometimes in jazz the soloist will play double time while the rhythm section continues as before.
double tonguing	A double tongue action that commences a note both with the outward and return stroke.
double whole note	*Breve.*
douleur (F)	Sadness.
doux, douce (F)	Sweet, soft.
downbeat	The downward beat of the conductor's hand or *baton*. The first beat of a measure.
Down Beat	Leading American jazz periodical, founded in 1934.

downstage	Front (audience side) of the stage.
doxologia, doxology	An 'expression of glory'. Any liturgical (Greek) form of praise.
drabant	An eighteenth century aristocratic Polish dance ceremony.
drag	A drum rudiment. A sticking pattern of two *grace notes* followed by two eighth notes. The second is accented.
Dragonetti	Palm-up bowing hold for double bass, named after Domenico Dragonetti (1763-1846), famous Italian double bass soloist.
dramatic soprano	A *soprano* voice suited to heavy dramatic roles. (See *lyric soprano*.)
drame lyrique (F)	One of several French names for *opera*.
dramma lirico (It)	Same as French *drame lyrique*.
dramma per musica (It)	Drama by music, or drama through music.
drammatico (It)	Dramatic.
drängend (G)	Urging forward, hurrying.
drawbars	The replacements for *stops* on some electric and electronic organs of the *Hammond* type, though drawbars have the advantage over stops, being variable in intensity.
Drehbühne (G)	Revolving stage.
Drehleier (G)	*Hurdy-gurdy.*
Drehorgel (G)	*Barrel organ.*
drei (G)	Three.
dreifach (G)	Threefold.
Dreiklang (G)	Triad.
dreinfahren (G)	To talk roughly.
dreitaktig (G)	'Three bar-ish'. In three measure phrases.
Dreivierteltakt (G)	Three-four time.
dringend (G)	Urgent.
dritte (G)	Third.
drohend (G)	Threatening.
droit, droite (F)	Right.
drone	A note (or notes) that sound continuously through a section of a performance, or even through a complete performance. In the case of bagpipes, the drones are usually tuned to the tonic of the key, or to the tonic and dominant. *Pedal point* is another type of drone, used as a section of a composition.
drop in	Recording new material onto a track that has already been recorded.

drucken (G)	To print.
drücken (G)	To press.
Druckfehler (G)	Printing error.
drum	Cylindrical percussion instrument with stretched skin or membrane over one (or both) ends. Struck with a stick, beater, wire *brushes* or bare hands.
drum and bass	Type of pop music in vogue at the end of the twentieth century, featuring repetitive drum and bass patterns, and little else.
drum kit	The dance band kit (as opposed to tuned percussion), which developed from the kits used by early jazz ensembles. These in turn were a 'sitting down' version of the percussion used for marching - a combination of *bass drum*, *snare drum*, *cymbals*, etc.
drum machine	An electronic means of providing digitally sampled drum sounds.
drumpad	1. A small practice pad, usually with a hard rubber surface. 2. Part of an electronic drum kit, the surface which responds to the impact of the drummer's sticks.
dry	A *dead* acoustic. Short reverberation time.
D.S.	*Dal Segno.*
du (F)	Of the.
dub	1. To record from a master tape, or the recording made from a master tape. 2. *Tabor.*
duda (Polish)	*Bagpipe.*
Dudelsack (G)	*Bagpipe.*
duduk	Flute-type instrument from Bulgaria, Yugoslavia and Turkey.
due (It)	Two.
duet	Any combination of two performers.
duftig (G)	Misty.
dulcimer	A shallow closed resonating box, over which are strung wires which are struck with hammers (*cimbalom*) or plucked with a plectrum (Appalachian dulcimer). *Hackbrett.*
dulcitone	A *céleste*, played from a keyboard, but with tuning forks as the sound-producing agents. *Gabelklavier.*
dumb keyboard	Silent piano keyboard, used for practice.
dumka	A somber Slavonic folk *ballad.*
dummy head	An artificial head, with the same dimensions as a

	human head, and with a pair of stereo microphones mounted at the ears. German: *Kunstkopf.*
dump, dumpe	A melancholy dance, about which little is known. Mentioned by Shakespeare.
dumpf (G)	Dull, muted.
dunkel (G)	Dark.
duo (It), (F)	*Duet.*
Duole (G)	*Duplet.*
duolo (It)	Grief. (Same as *dolore.*)
duple meter	A time signature with two beats to a measure.
duplet	A group of two notes to be performed in the time of three.
duplex instruments	Brass instruments which are provided with two bells or two sets of mechanism. The trumpeter Bobby Shew performs on an instrument of this type, which he calls a Shew Horn.
Dur (G)	Major.
dur (F)	Hard.
duramente (It)	Harshness, sternness.
durch (G)	Through.
durchaus (G)	Throughout.
durchdringend (G)	Through-forcing, penetrating, shrill.
Durchführung (G)	Through-leading. Development.
durchkomponiert (G)	Through-composed, continuous. The music is different for each section, not merely a repeated tune. Applies to songs.
durchweg (G)	Throughout, on the whole, nearly always.
dureté (F)	Hardness, severity.
durezza (It)	Hardness, severity.
duro (It)	Hard, firm.
düster (G)	Somber.
duttile, trombone (It)	Slide trombone.
dynamic	Loudness, intensity.
dynamic range	The difference between the loudest and quietest parts of a performance.
Dynamik (G)	*Dynamics.*

E

e, ed (It)	And.
early music	Term to describe European music from the Middle Ages to the mid-eighteenth century.
earphones	Headphones.
ear training	Course that teaches how to hear music and write it down.
easy listening	Music marketing term for middle-of-the-road (*MOR*) light music or background music.
ebenfalls (G)	Likewise.
ebenso (G)	Just as.
échappée (F)	*Escaped note*. Changing note.
échelette (F)	*Xylophone*.
échelle (F)	*Scale*. The more common name for scale is *gamme*.
echo (Eng), **eco** (It)	An imitation of a previous passage, usually quieter.
echo chamber	A room used to create reverberation effects.
éclatant (F)	Brilliant, gorgeous. Also piercing.
eclogue	A short pastoral poem.
école (F)	School.
écossaise (F)	Said to be a dance of Scottish origin, though the écossaises of Beethoven, Schubert and Chopin seem to have no Scottish characteristics.
edel (G)	Noble.
editing	Process of altering a recording.
effects	Devices that change the characteristics of an audio signal, to produce *chorus, compression, delay, distortion, echo, equalization, flanging, limiting, reverb*, etc.
effects board, effects pedal (jazz)	Plectrum guitarists have many electronic ways to modify or color the sound they produce. This additional circuitry is usually fitted into small boxes, and is foot-operated, using a pedal. To avoid clutter and aid portability these effects are frequently mounted together onto a common chassis - an effects board.
effleurer (F)	To touch very lightly.
égal (F), **eguale** (It)	Equal.
églogue (F)	*Eclogue*.
Eifer (G)	Zeal, heat.
eifrig (G)	Zealous.

eight (jazz)	Eight bars.
eighth, eighth note	A note one eighth the duration of a whole note. *Quaver.*
eights	Exchange of eight-measure improvised passages in jazz improvisation. This may then proceed to fours, and even to twos.
Eile (G)	Haste.
eilen (G)	To rush, to hasten.
eilig (G)	Speedy.
ein, eine (G)	One, a.
einfach (G)	Simple, single.
Eingang (G)	Entrance (of building).
Einhalt (G)	A pause.
einige (G)	Some, a few.
Einklang (G)	*Unison*, harmony.
Einleitung (G)	Introduction.
einlenken (G)	To turn back.
einmal (G)	Once.
Einsatz (G)	*Cue* (music).
Einsingzimmer (G)	Warm-up room.
einstimmig (G)	One-voiced. Monodic.
einstudieren (G)	To coach, rehearse.
Eintritt (G)	Entrance, beginning.
ein wenig (G)	A little.
einzeln (G)	Single.
Eis (G)	E sharp.
eiserner Vorhang (G)	Safety curtain.
Eisis (G)	E double sharp.
élan (F)	Dash, impetuosity.
élargir, élargissant (F)	To broaden.
electric bass	A four-string solid body *electric guitar*, tuned as a bass.
electric guitar	A guitar fitted with electronics to amplify the sound.
electro-acoustic music	A combination of electronic music and 'natural' sounds that may or may not have been processed electronically. An art music, whose leading exponents have included Babbitt, Stockhausen and Varèse.
electronic music	Music from electronically generated sound.
elegantemente (It)	Elegantly.
élégie (F), **elegiaco** (It)	*Elegy*, elegiac.
elegy	A work of lamentation for the dead.

Elevatio (L), **Elevation**	Music performed during the Elevation of the Host in the Roman Catholic Church.
elevato (It)	Elevated.
elevazione (It)	Elevation.
élève (F)	Pupil.
eleventh	The interval of an eleventh. Eleven notes.
éloigner (F)	To put farther away.
embellishment	A musical *ornament*.
embouchure	The area of the face involved with the playing of a wind instrument. Includes lips, teeth and cheeks, and the surrounding muscles. See *chops*.
emozione (It)	Emotion.
Empfindung (G)	Emotion, feeling, sentiment.
empfindungsvoll (G)	With feeling.
emporté (F)	Fiery, impetuous, carried away.
empressé (F)	Eager.
ému (F)	Moved.
en (F)	In, whilst.
en animant (F)	Becoming more lively.
en cédant (F)	Yielding.
enchaînez (F)	Join up, play the next movement without a break.
enclume (F)	*Anvil.*
encore	Again.
en dehors (F)	Outside, prominent. Bring out a melody.
energia (It)	Energy.
energico (It)	Energetic.
enfasi (It)	Emphasis.
enfatico, enfaticamente (It)	Emphatic, emphatically.
Engelstimme (G)	'Angel voice'. The vox angelica stop on the organ.
Englischhorn (G)	*English horn. Cor anglais.*
English horn	An alto *oboe*, pitched a fifth lower (in F). Has a conical bore and a distinctive bulbous bell.
enharmonic	Two notes that are the same pitch but described differently, such as A sharp and B flat.
enigmatic scale	C, D♭, E, F sharp, G sharp, A sharp, B, C ascending. The F sharp changes to F natural when descending.
enlevez (F)	Take up, take off. A direction for a pedal or a mute.
en mesure (F)	In time.
en pressant (F)	Hurrying on.
en retenant (F)	Holding back. Slowing.
ensemble	French for 'together'. Group of instrumentalists or singers.

en serrant (F)	Becoming quicker.
entendre (F)	To hear.
entfernt (G)	Distant.
entr'acte (F)	Music played between acts.
entrada (Sp)	*Entrée. Prelude.*
entrain (F)	Vigor, dash, go.
entrata (It)	Entrance, beginning.
entrée	A sub-division of an act (a scene or section) in an opera or ballet.
entremés (Sp)	A comic musical *intermezzo* in a play.
Entrückung (G)	The state of absence, hence rapture. 'Transported' is 'entrückt'.
entrudo (P)	Boisterous style of celebrating *Carnaval* that originated in Portugal and was popular in Brazil until the mid-nineteenth century.
entschieden (G)	Decided, resolute.
entschlossen (G)	Determined.
entusiasmo (It)	Enthusiasm.
envelope	In *synthesis*, the shape of some aspect of the sound (such as volume) over time.
episode	A subsidiary section. In a *fugue*, a section that does not contain the main theme or *subject*. In *rondo* form, a contrasting passage.
epithalamium	A marriage song.
éponge, baguette d' (F)	Sponge-headed drumstick.
EQ	**EQ**ualizer, equalization.
equabile (It)	Equable.
equale (It)	Short pieces (usually for four trombones) played during an Austrian funeral.
equalization	In amplification, the process of setting a tonal balance.
equal temperament	A tuning system that divides the octave into equal intervals.
équivaut (F)	Is equivalent to.
ergriffen (G)	Gripped, emotionally moved.
erhaben (G)	Sublime.
Erleichterung (G)	Easing. A simplified version.
erlöschend (G)	Becoming weaker.
Ermangelung (G)	Default.
ermattend, ermattet (G)	Becoming tired out, tired out.
erniedrigen (G)	To lower (pitch).
ernst, ernsthaft (G)	Earnest, serious.
eroico, eroica (It)	Heroic.

Ersatz (G)	Substitute.
erschüttert (G)	Shaken, agitated.
erst, erste (G)	First.
Erstaufführung	First performance.
ersterbend (G)	Dying away.
erster Rang (G)	Dress circle.
erstickt (G)	Suffocated, stifled.
erweitert (G)	Widened, broadened.
erzürnt (G)	Irritated. Angered.
Es (G)	E flat.
esaltato (It)	Excited, exalted.
esatto, esatta (It)	Exact.
escape tone,	A nonharmonic note between two notes,
escaped note	which takes a step in one direction, then a leap (of at least a third) in the other direction.
escola de samba (P)	Body that organizes samba parades during *Carnaval*. Typically, it has many other social functions.
esecuzione (It)	Execution.
esercizio, esercizi (It)	Exercise, exercises.
Eses (G)	E double flat.
esotico, esotica (It)	Exotic.
Espagne (F)	Spain.
espagnol, espagnole (F)	Spanish.
espagnolo, espagnuolo, espagnola, espagnuola (It)	Spanish.
espirando (It)	Expiring, dying away.
espressione (It)	Expression.
espressivo, espress., espr. (It)	Expressive.
esquisse (F)	Sketch.
estinguendo (It)	Extinguishing.
estinto (It)	As soft as possible, lifeless.
estompé (F)	Toned down.
estravaganza (It)	Extravagance.
estremamente (It)	Extremely.
estudiantino, estudiantina (Sp)	In the spirit or style of a party of students.
esultazione (It)	Exultation.
et (F), (L)	And.
éteindre (F)	To extinguish.
étendue (F)	Extent, compass, *range*.

ethnomusicology	The study of types of music in relation to their anthropological background.
étouffer (F)	To damp, stifle.
étude	French for *study*. A composition intended for the improvement of technical skill.
etwas (G)	Somewhat, rather.
euchorics	Verse-speaking in chorus.
Euphonion (G), **euphonium** (Eng)	A member of the *tuba* family.
eurhythmics, eurhythmy	A system of teaching rhythm through body movements, founded and developed by Émile Jaques-Dalcroze (1865-1950).
éveillé (F)	Awakened.
even (jazz)	Eighth notes (quavers) that are not swung or bounced, i.e. they are played evenly.
Evensong	The Anglican service of evening prayer. In the Roman Catholic Church it was formerly a synonym for *Vespers*.
evirato (It)	'Unmanned'. Refers to a *castrato* singing in a higher voice.
evocación (Sp)	Evocation, invocation.
exactement (F)	Exactly.
exalté (F)	Exalted, very excited.
exposition	**1.** The (initial) part of a movement of *sonata form* wherein the main themes are stated, before they are developed. **2.** The (initial) statement of the subject of a *fugue*, wherein all the voices are heard in turn.
expressif (F)	Expressive.
expressionism	Name used originally to describe a group of early twentieth century painters, including Kandinsky and the composer Arnold Schoenberg, and applied to literature, drama and music.
expression marks	Instructions for musical performance, such as *articulation*, *dynamics*, mood and *tempo*.
extemporization	Synonym for *improvisation*, most often used in a non-jazz context.
extensions	The higher intervals of a chord, above the seventh, e.g. ninth, eleventh and thirteenth, and chromatic alterations of these.
extravaganza	Nineteenth century English light entertainment, on stage, with music.
extrêmement (F)	Extremely.

F

f	Abbreviation of *forte*, loud.
fa	Fourth degree of major scale.
faburden (Eng),	False bass. Adding an extra voice or voices in
fauxbourdon (F),	counterpoint to a given chant, (fifteenth century).
falsobordone (It)	The practice varied in different countries.
fach (G)	Fold, as in two fold, five fold.
Fachpartie (G)	Principal role.
facile (F), (It)	Easy.
facilement (F),	Easily, fluently.
facilmente (It)	
facilità (It)	Facility.
Fackeltanz (G)	Torch dance.
fader	On a *mixing* desk, the control on one channel for adjusting the level of that channel relative to the others.
fado (P)	Portuguese song, usually melancholy, with guitar accompaniment. 'Fate'.
Fagott (G)	*Bassoon.*
fagotto (It)	*Bassoon.*
fahren (G)	To go.
faible (F)	Feeble, weak.
faire (F)	To do, to make.
faites (F)	Do, make. (Imperative case.)
fake	To play by ear (without music), to *busk.*
fake book	A book containing *standard* songs, in an abbreviated form, usually *top line* and *chord symbols* only.
fall	*Cadence.*
fall (jazz)	A rapid descending run of notes of indeterminate pitch, quickly fading away.
Fall, Falle (G)	Case. As in: 'in this case', 'in this instance'.
false fingering	An alternative fingering, usually on woodwind instruments, to give a different tone quality or *intonation.*
false relation	Where the relationship between parts in harmony writing is such that a chromatically altered note appearing in one part disagrees with that note, unaltered, following closely in another part.
falsetto (It)	A high artificial voice. The head voice in adults.
fancy	Same as *fantasia.*

fandango	Lively Spanish dance for a single couple.
fandanguilla	A sort of *fandango*.
fanfare	A flourish of trumpets. In French the term means brass band.
fantaisie (F)	Fantasia. A piece free in style and form.
fantasia	Italian for fancy.
Fantasiestück (G)	Fantasy.
fantastico (It),	Fantastic, whimsical.
fantasque (F),	
fantastisch (G)	
fantasy	A piece free in style and form.
farandole (F)	A French line dance from Provence, in 6/8 time.
Farbe (G)	Color.
farruca	Andalusian dance of gypsy origin.
Fassung (G)	Setting, version, draft.
fast (G)	Almost.
fastoso (It)	Pompous.
fausset (F)	*Falsetto.*
feedback	In amplification or *sound reinforcement*, the (normally unintentional) return of the output to the input. Thus a microphone may pick up the sound from a loudspeaker, resulting in a harsh squeal.
feierlich (G)	Solemn. Festive. (Public celebration, holiday or Holy Day.)
felice (It)	Happy.
Fell (G)	Skin (of a drum).
feminine cadence	A *cadence* resolving onto a weak beat.
Fender	An American guitar manufacturing company, famous for their bass instruments. Term used to distinguish the electric *bass guitar* from the upright acoustic bass.
Fender-Rhodes	See *Rhodes piano*.
fermamente (It)	Firmly.
fermata (It), **Fermate** (G)	Pause.
ferme (F)	Firm.
fermer (F)	To close.
fermezza (It)	Firmness.
fermo (It)	Firm.
Fernwerk (G)	Echo manual of an organ.
feroce (It)	Fierce.
fertig (G)	Finished (in style), ready.
fervente (It)	Fervent.
fervido,	Fervid.
fervidamente (It)	

fervore (It)	Fervor.
Fes (G)	F flat.
Feses (G)	F double flat.
Fest (G)	Festival.
festa (It)	Festival.
festivo (It)	Festive.
festlich (G)	Festive, solemn, splendid.
festoso (It)	Festive.
Festspiel (G)	Festival play.
Feuer (G)	Fire.
feuille d' album (F)	Album leaf. See *Albumblatt*.
feurig (G)	Fiery.
ff	Abbreviation of *fortissimo*, very loud.
fff	Abbreviation of *fortississimo,* very very loud.
f holes	Sound holes in the belly of some guitars, viols and members of the violin family.
fiacco (It)	Weak.
fiata, fiate (It)	Time, times.
fiato (It)	Breath.
fiddle	*Violin.* Sometimes used of other bowed string instruments.
Fidel, Fiedel (G)	*Fiddle.*
fier, fière (F)	Proud.
fierezza (It)	Fierceness.
fiero (It)	Fierce, fiery. Haughty.
fife	Small high-pitched wooden flute, of *piccolo* size, usually without keys.
fifth	An interval of five steps (i.e. five letter-names) in the diatonic major or minor scale.
figure	A short musical phrase.
figured bass	Shorthand system of harmony, used from seventeenth century onwards by keyboard and *continuo* players. Also known as *thoroughbass* and *basso continuo*.
filar la voce (It), **filer le son** (F), **spinnen des Tons** (G)	'Draw out the voice'. Sustain for a long time.
fill (jazz)	Instruction to an accompanist or a jazz instrumentalist to play answering phrases in the spaces between phrases sung or played by a soloist.
filter	An electronic device that boosts or cuts certain frequencies or waveforms. Used in *synthesis*.

fin (F)	End.
finale	**1.** The final movement of a work in several movements.
	2. An ensemble ending an *opera*.
finaon	Music from Cape Verde Islands. See also *batuco*.
fine (It)	End.
fingerboard	Long piece of hardwood on a stringed instrument above which the strings are stretched, and onto which the fingers press.
finger cymbals	Small pairs of *cymbals* that are worn on the fingers.
fingering	**1.** Notation written on music to specify which fingers to use.
	2. The act of placing the fingers.
fingerpicking	*Guitar* and *banjo* technique, plucking the strings with each individual finger. See *flatpicking*.
Fingersatz (G)	*Fingering.*
fino (It)	As far as.
fioritura (It)	Flowering. Embellishment of a melodic line.
fipple	The plug at the mouth of an end-blown wind instrument, which channels the air towards the window.
first inversion	A chord with the third as its lowest note. Six-three chord.
Fis (G)	F sharp.
fish horn (jazz)	Soprano *saxophone*. Refers to the straight version, not the curved one.
Fisis (G)	F double sharp.
Five, The	Group of five nineteenth century Russian composers: Balakirev, Borodin, Cui, Mussorgsky and Rimsky-Korsakov.
five-three chord	Root position *triad*.
fixer	Person who hires musicians on behalf of the individual or body financing an engagement.
flag	The tail on the right-hand side of the stem of a note. Indicates an eighth note or smaller.
flageolet	Six-holed end-blown wind instrument, an obsolete type of *recorder*.
flageolet notes	The *harmonics* of the *violin*, the name referring to the thin sound, which is reminiscent of the thin sound of the *flageolet*.
Flageolett (G)	Harmonic. **Künstliches Flageolett** = artificial harmonic.
flag-waver (jazz)	A piece, usually an arrangement for *big band* or

jazz orchestra, that is loud, celebratory and attention-getting. Frequently placed at the beginning or end of a performance. (See *opener* and *shout chorus*.)

flam A two note rudiment in drumming. A small *grace note* played softly before the written note, with alternate sticking.

flamenco The traditional music of Andalusia in Southern Spain, including song, dance and solo guitar. The flamenco style in guitar playing is forceful, and with a different instrument and technique from that used in classical guitar.

flanging A type of electronic sound treatment. Owes its name to the distortion created by holding an object against (or touching) the flange of a rotating tape spool, thus unsteadying the playback speed.

flat 1. Sign placed before a note, lowering it in pitch by half a tone.
2. Below pitch

flatpicking On *guitar* or *banjo*, string plucking using a *plectrum* (pick).

flatter (F) To caress.

Flatterzunge, Flzg. (G) *Flutter-tongue.*

flautato, flautando (It) Flute-like. A direction for natural *harmonics* on string instruments.

flautist British spelling of *flutist*.

flauto (It) *Flute.*

flauto dolce (It) Sweet flute. *Recorder. Blockflöte.*

flebile, flebilmente (It) Mournful, mournfully.

flehend (G) Entreating.

flessibile (It) Flexible. Not in strict time.

Flexatone Commercial name for a hand-held percussion instrument having a small tempered-steel plate against which a pair of integral hard beaters are struck.

flies The area high above the stage, the place to which scenery is lifted or 'flown'.

fliessend, (fließend) (G) Flowing.

fling Scottish dance, a lively type of *reel*.

Flöte (G) *Flute.*

Flötenspieler (G) *Flutist.*

flottant (F) Floating.

flotter (F) To float.

flourish	A *fanfare*.
flüchtig (G)	Fleeting.
fluff	Wrong note.
Flügel (G)	Grand piano.
flugelhorn	A conical bore brass instrument in B♭, similar in size and shape to the trumpet. Distinguished by its wider body and *bell*, and mellower sound.
Flügelhorn (G)	*Flugelhorn.*
fluido (It)	Fluid.
flüssig (G)	Fluid.
flüstern (G)	To whisper.
flute	**1.** General name for various types of wind instruments without reeds. **2.** Specific name for a transverse-blown orchestral woodwind instrument, nowadays usually made of metal. It has a cylindrical body, closed at one end, and the range is around three octaves.
flûte (F)	*Flute.*
flûté (F)	*Flautando.*
flûte à bec (F)	Beak flute. *Recorder. Blockflöte.*
flûte harmonique (F)	*Mouth organ.*
flutist	Flute player. *Flautist.*
flutter-tonguing	A rapid 'buzz' introduced to the sound of a woodwind instrument by rolling the tongue and saying "rrr". *Flatterzunge.*
FM	Frequency Modulation.
FM synthesis	*Synthesis* in which wave forms interact to produce complex timbres.
focoso (It)	Fiery.
fofa (P)	Voluptuous eighteenth century Portuguese dance.
fois (F)	Time.
foldback	Headphones (or a loudspeaker positioned near to a performer, facing away from the audience) to allow the performer to hear his or her own performance clearly.
Folge (G)	Succession, series.
folgen (G)	To follow.
folk rock	A mixture of folk music and *rock 'n' roll.*
folk song	Strictly, songs or music passed down through oral tradition, with no composer traceable. Traditional music that reflects a regional or national characteristic. Modern usage sometimes includes songs that have become widely accepted, such as those of Stephen Foster.

fonds d'orgue (F)	Foundation stops of the organ.
forlana (It), **forlane** (F)	Old Italian dance, six in a measure.
format de poche (F)	Pocket-size.
fort (G)	Forwards, away.
forte, *f* (It)	Loud, strong.
fortepiano, *fp* (It)	1. Instruction to play loud, then immediately soft.
	2. Historic name applied to the early *pianoforte*.
fortfahren (G)	To go forward.
fortissimo, *ff* (It)	Very loud.
fortississimo, *fff* (It)	Very, very loud.
Fortsetzung (G)	Continuation.
Forty-Eight, The	Popular name for Bach's 'The Well-Tempered Clavier' (BWV 846 - 893).
forza (It)	Force.
forzando, forzato (It)	Forced. Strongly accented.
fougueux, fougueuse (F)	Impetuous.
fours (jazz)	Four-measure exchanges between improvising musicians.
fourth	An interval of four steps (i.e. four letter-names) in the diatonic major or minor scale.
fourth chord	A chord built of intervals of a fourth. See *quartal harmony*.
foxtrot	A ballroom dance of American origin, in 4/4 time, popular from the period of the First World War.
frailich (Yiddish)	Lively East European Jewish dance in 2/4 time.
franc (F)	Open hearted, bluff.
français, française (F)	French.
française (F)	A nineteenth century round dance in triple or compound duple time.
franchezza (It), **franchise** (F)	Freedom of spirit, boldness.
frapper (F)	To strike.
Frauenchor (G)	Women's choir.
fredonner (F)	To hum.
free jazz	A style of jazz of the fifties and sixties that is, allegedly, free. That is, it has no set time signature, form or harmonic scheme (no *time* or *changes*). Thus, paradoxically, it is not truly free.
free reed	A reed that vibrates freely, such as in a *reed organ*, *mouth organ* or *accordion*, as opposed to the controlled reed in a *clarinet* or *oboe*.

frei (G)	Free, (*ganz frei* - totally free).
French horn	Coiled brass orchestral instrument with a flared bell and valves.
French overture	An instrumental form from the *Baroque* era, featuring a slow first section with dotted rhythms, followed by a fast section with a fugal texture.
French sixth	A type of *augmented sixth* chord, for example in the key of C on the flattened supertonic, with the intervals (reading upwards) D♭, F, G, B. See *German sixth* and *Italian sixth*. The origins of these names are not known.
frenetico, frenetica (It)	Frenzied.
fresco (It)	Fresh, cool.
fretboard	*Fingerboard.*
frets	Raised strips across the *fingerboard* of a stringed instrument, to mark the location of the pitch.
fretta (It)	Haste.
Freude (G)	Joy.
freudig (G)	Joyful.
friction drum	A drum in which a rod or a cord is attached to the center of the head, and the sound is produced by the friction between the performer's hand and the rod or cord. The drumhead amplifies the sound. See *cuíca*.
frigideira (P)	Brazilian percussion instrument, shaped like a frying pan, played with a stick.
frisch (G)	Fresh, vigorous.
frog	The end of a (violin, etc.) *bow* that is held in the hand.
fröhlich (G)	Cheerful, joyful, happy.
froid (F)	Cold.
from the edge	From the beginning.
from the top	From the beginning.
front line	Melody instruments. Usually refers to the wind instruments in a jazz *combo*.
Frosch (G)	The *frog*, *nut* or *heel* of the *bow* of the *violin*. The end held by the hand.
frottola, frottole (It)	Popular unaccompanied choral form, c.1500.
frug	1960s dance style.
früher (G)	Earlier, previous.
Frühlingslied (G)	Spring song.
fuga (It), (L)	A *fugue*. Flight.
fugato (It)	A passage in fugal style.

Fuge (G)	*Fugue.*
fughetta (It)	A short *fugue.*
fugue	'Flight.' A *contrapuntal* composition for two or more parts (or 'voices'). Voices enter successively in imitation of each other.
führend (G)	Leading.
full close	*Perfect cadence.*
Füllflöte (G)	Full-toned flute stop on the organ.
Fülligstimmen (G)	'Full-toned voices'. Organ stops of loud tone.
full score	*Score* for full orchestra, in which all the instrumental parts are displayed in a standard order.
Füllstimme (G)	**1.** *Ripieno.* 'Filling voice'.
	2. The mixture stop of an organ.
fundamental	The lowest note in a *harmonic series.*
funèbre (F), **funebre** (It)	Funeral.
fünf (G)	Five.
funk, funky	A term that originally meant 'smelly'. Later came to mean groovy, hip, blues-drenched and intense.
fuoco (It)	Fire.
für (G)	For.
furia (It)	Fury.
furiant	Bohemian dance, with rapid tempo and changing rhythms.
furieux, furieusement (F)	Furious, furiously.
furioso (It)	Furious.
furore (It)	Fury, rage, passion.
furry dance	Ancient folk dance, associated with Helston in Cornwall, England, and performed to celebrate the coming of spring.
fusion	Musical style that emerged in the 1970s and 1980s, combining ('fusing') elements of jazz with a rhythmic approach heavily influenced by rock.
fuyant (F)	Fleeing.
fuzzbox, fuzz pedal, fuzz tone	An electronic attachment that modifies (distorts) the sound of an electric guitar to give it a growling tone.
fz	*Forzando, sforzando.*

G

G — *Grand orgue*, meaning 'great organ'.

Gabelklavier (G) — 'Fork-keyboard'. *Dulcitone.*

gagaku (Japanese) — Traditional Japanese court orchestral music, with percussion, strings and wind.

Gage (G), **Honorar** (G) — Fee.

gagliarda (It) — *Galliard.*

gai, gaiement (F) — Gay, gaily.

gain — The amount of amplification given to a signal by a piece of equipment. Measured in decibels.

gaio, gaia (It) — Gay.

galant, galamment (F) — Gallant, gallantly.

Galanterien (G), **galanteries** (F) — Movements of a classical *suite* which are not essential to the scheme.

Galerie (G) — Gallery.

galliard — Sixteenth and early seventeenth century lively court dance in triple meter, often paired with the more stately *pavan.*

galop — Energetic nineteenth century dance in 2/4 time.

gamba — 'Leg'. *Viola da gamba.*

Gambe (G) — *Viol, viola da gamba.*

gamelan — Indonesian (Java, Bali) percussion ensemble. Has influenced many Western composers, including Debussy, Glass and Reich.

gamme (F) — *Scale.*

gamut — **1.** *Compass, range.*
2. The note G at the bottom of the *bass clef.*

gangar — A Norwegian walking dance.

ganz (G) — Whole, entire (totally, complete).

ganzá (P) — Single, double or triple tubular metal shaker. A wooden or metal square with cymbals. (Brazilian.)

Ganze Pause (G) — Whole note (semibreve) rest.

Ganztaktnote (G) — Whole measure note.

gapped scale — Scale containing leaps as well as steps - such as the *pentatonic* scale.

garage — Type of simple pop music, so named because of the rehearsal locations.

garbo (It) — Manners.

garder (F) — To keep, to hold.

Garderobe (G), **Künstlergarderobe** (G) — Dressing room, artists' dressing room.

Gassenhauer (G)	Street song.
gastieren (G)	To tour.
Gastspiel (G)	Guest performance.
gauche (F)	Left.
gaúcho, gaúcha (P)	Someone or something from Rio Grande do Sul state, Brazil.
gavotte	Old dance in 4/4 time, beginning on the third beat of the bar. Sometimes part of the *Baroque suite*.
G clef	*Treble clef.*
Gebläse (G)	Wind supply (organ).
Gebrauchsmusik (G)	Music for use. Music for the everyday, for social or educational purposes.
gebrochen (G)	Divided, *divisi*.
gebunden (G)	Joined, bound, tied, *legato*, fretted.
gedämpft (G)	Damped, muffled, muted.
gedeckt (G)	Covered, muted, stopped.
gedehnt (G)	Stretched out, sustained.
Gedicht (G)	Poem.
Gefallen (G)	Pleasure.
gefällig (G)	Agreeable.
Gefühl (G)	Feeling.
gegen (G)	Against, counter, towards.
gehalten (G)	Held out.
gehaucht (G)	Whispered.
geheimnisvoll (G)	Mysterious, secretive.
gehend (G)	'Going', at a steady speed, (literally 'walking', like *andante*).
Gehör (G)	Hearing. Ear (for music).
Gehörbildung (G)	Aural training.
gehörig (G)	Proper, suitable.
Geige (G)	*Violin*. Originally any bowed instrument.
Geigenbauer (G)	*Violin* maker.
Geiger (G)	Violinist, fiddler.
Geist (G)	Spirit, soul.
geistlich (G)	Spiritual.
gekkin	Japanese *lute*.
gekneipt (G)	Plucked, *pizzicato*.
gekoppelt (G)	Coupled.
gelassen (G)	Calm, tranquil.
geläufig (G)	Fluent, nimble.
Geläufigkeit (G)	Fluency.
Geläute (G)	Peal of bells.
gemächlich (G)	Comfortable, unhurried.

gemässigt, **(gemäßigt)** (G)	Moderate, moderate tempo.
gemendo, gemebondo (It)	Moaning, lamenting.
gemessen (G)	Measured.
Gemüt (G)	Feeling.
gemütlich (G)	Easy going, comfortable.
genannt (G)	Called, known as.
genau (G)	Exact, exactly.
Generalbass, **(Generalbaß)** (G)	*Thoroughbass*, *continuo*.
general pause	Rest or pause for everyone. *Grand pause.* Sometimes abbreviated to G.P.
Generalprobe (G)	Dress rehearsal, final rehearsal.
generoso (It)	Generous, grand in style.
gentil, gentille (F)	Gentle, pleasant, pretty.
gentile (It)	Gentle, delicate.
German sixth	A type of *augmented sixth* chord built on the flattened supertonic (i.e. the minor second of the scale). For example, in the key of C it would be (reading upwards) D♭, F, A♭, B. See *French sixth*, *Italian sixth*.
Gershwin tenth	A dominant seventh chord which contains both a major third and a flattened third (the tenth) above.
gerührt (G)	Moved (emotionally).
Ges (G)	G flat.
Gesangverein (G)	Choral society.
gesangvoll (G)	In a singing style (like *cantabile*).
geschlagen (G)	Struck.
geschleift (G)	Slurred, *legato*.
geschlossen (G)	Closed.
Geschmack (G)	Taste.
geschmackvoll (G)	Tastefully.
geschwind (G)	Quick.
Geses (G)	G double flat.
gesprochen (G)	Spoken.
gesteigert (G)	Increased, *crescendo*.
gestopft (G)	Stopped notes in *horn* playing.
gestossen, **(gestoßen)** (G)	Pushed away, detached, *staccato*.
getheilt, geteilt (G)	Divided. As *divisi*.
getragen (G)	Carried, sustained.
Gewandmeisterin (G)	Wardrobe mistress.
gewichtig (G)	Weightily.

gewidmet (G)	Dedicated.
gewöhnlich (G)	Usual.
gezogen (G)	Drawn. Either (a) drawn out, or (b) the same as *portamento*.
ghetto blaster	A large portable tape recorder plus radio.
ghiribizzo (It)	*Caprice.*
ghosted, ghost notes	Notes which are implied rather than played. In a jazz score they are notated by using a cross for the note head.
gig	Musician's term which originally meant 'casual engagement'. It has now been borrowed by the would-be hip, from DJs and broadcasters to comedians, referring to work or performances of any kind.
gigue (F)	*Jig.* Lively dance, usually in 6/8 or 12/8 time. Said to originate in the British Isles. Frequently included as the last item in the *Baroque suite*.
giocoso (It)	Playful, humorous.
gioioso (It)	Joyful, merry.
gioviale (It)	Jovial.
Gis (G)	G sharp.
Gisis (G)	G double sharp.
gitano, gitana (Sp)	Gypsy.
giù (It)	Down.
giubilo, giubilio (It)	Joy.
giulivo (It)	Joyous.
giuoco (It)	Play, game.
giustamente (It)	Exactly.
giusto (It)	Proper, exact.
glam-rock	Form of rock music with a message of sexual decadence, in which dress and make-up are more important than the music.
glänzend (G)	Brilliant.
glass harmonica	Rubbing a moistened finger around the rim of a glass bowl produces an ethereal note. The glass harmonica is a collection of different sized bowls, either arranged flat on a table, or mounted together on an axle, rotated by the performer.
glass master	A glass disc, used as an intermediate stage in the process of producing a CD.
glatt (G)	Smooth.
glee	*Partsong* for unaccompanied male voices, English in origin and harmonic rather than contrapuntal in style. Flourished between 1750-1830.

gleich (G)	Like.
gleichmässig (G)	Evenly.
gleitend (G)	Gliding.
gli (It)	The.
glide	*Portamento, glissando.* A smooth slide between notes.
glissando, gliss. (It)	Slide.
glitch	Unexpected (and unwanted) event.
global music	*World music.*
Glöckchen (G)	Small bell.
Glocke(n) (G)	Orchestral tubular bells.
Glockenspiel (G)	A small tuned percussion instrument, with steel bars laid out in the pattern of a keyboard, and struck with mallets.
glühend (G)	Glowing.
gobstick, gobbo	Obsolete jazz-slang term for the *clarinet*. *Blackstick, licorice stick*, stick o' licorice.
go-go	Exciting, plentiful.
go-go dancer	Girl hired to dance in a disco, often on a bar or in a cage.
going up, go up	When the curtain goes up. The time of the start of a performance, as in 'What time do we go up?'
golden oldie	Old hit pop record.
gold record	A record that has sold a large quantity. The specific amount defining 'gold' status diminishes as record sales decline.
gong	Circular percussion instrument, originally from the Orient, made of sheet bronze, usually with a turned-down edge.
goofus	A novelty instrument famously associated with jazz saxophonist Adrian Rollini in the 1920s. Each key controls a reed, so that it can produce chords. Also known as a 'Couesnophone', after the French company Couesnon, which manufactured it.
gopak	Lively Russian dance.
gorgheggio (It)	Long rapid vocal passage in which one vowel takes many notes.
gospel	Popular Christian music.
G. P.	*General pause.*
grace note	A decoration, an ornamental note played quickly before the beat, and notated smaller than the main note.
gracieux (F)	Graceful.

gradatamente (It)	Gradually.
gradevole (It)	Pleasing.
gradito (It)	Pleasant.
graduellement (F)	Gradually.
gran (It)	Great, big.
granadina	A kind of *fandango*. Southern Spanish dance from Granada, Andalusia.
gran cassa (It)	'Big box'. Bass drum.
grand, grande (F)	Great, large.
grand choeur (F)	Full choir.
grandezza (It)	Grandeur, dignity.
grandioso (It)	Grandly.
grandisonante (It)	Sonorous.
grand jeu (F)	Full organ.
grand opera	Strictly, *opera* in which the *libretto* is entirely set to music.
grand orchestre (F)	Full orchestra, large orchestra.
grand orgue (F)	Full organ, great organ.
grand pause	*General pause. G.P.*
grand piano	Piano with a horizontal wing-shaped case, strings and soundboard.
grand staff (or **stave**)	Combination of the treble and bass staves.
gran gusto (It)	Great taste.
gran tamburo (It)	Big drum. Bass drum.
grave (It), (F)	Very slow, solemn.
gravement (F),	Gravely.
gravemente (It)	
gravicembalo (It)	Term used for newly invented piano of Bartolomeo Cristofori, early eighteenth century.
gravità (It)	Gravity, seriousness.
grazia, grazioso,	Grace, graceful, gracefully.
graziosamente (It)	
graziös (G)	Gracious, graceful.
great staff, great stave	*Grand staff.*
Gregorian chant	A type of *plainsong* associated with Saint Gregory (540 - 604, Pope 590-604).
grelots (F)	Little bells, sleigh bells.
Griff (G)	Grip, anything gripped. Barring (guitar).
Griffbrett (G)	*Fingerboard.*
Griffloch (G)	Finger hole.
grimmig (G)	Grim, furious.
groaning stick	*Thunder stick.*
grob (G)	Coarse, rough.

groove	Swinging empathy. Cohesion.
gros, grosse (F)	Great, big.
gross, grosse (G)	Great, large.
grosse caisse (F)	'Big box'. Bass drum.
großer Dreiklang (G)	Major *triad.*
grosses Orchester (G)	Full orchestra.
große Trommel (G)	Bass drum.
gros tambour (F)	Great drum.
grotesk (G)	Grotesque.
ground, ground bass	A bass figure that is repeated persistently throughout a piece, with changing upper parts.
groupie	A girl who follows rock groups.
growl	An effect used by wind instrumentalists, (particularly in jazz) when the player growls in his throat as he plays, thus coloring or 'dirtying' the tone.
Grundgestalt (G)	*Prime,* in serialism.
Grundreihe (G)	The row on which a twelve-note composition is based.
Grundstimmen (G)	Ground voices. The foundation stops of an organ.
Grundton (G)	*Tonic, keynote.*
gruppetto (It)	*Turn.* ('Small group' - originally a *trill.*)
G string	The lowest string on a *violin.*
guajira	Cuban folk dance, traditionally alternating rhythms of 3/4 and 6/8. See *joropa.*
guaracha, guarracha	Latin-American dance rhythm, influenced by the *habanera.*
guerre des bouffons	'War of the Comedians', or 'Buffoons'.
guerriero, guerriera (It)	Warlike.
Guidonian hand	Named after Guido d'Arezzo, an eleventh century Italian monk, who invented this memory aid in which the fingers are given the names of various notes. A form of *solmization.*
guimbarde (F)	*Jew's harp.*
güiro	Latin-American percussion instrument, a notched bamboo tube or a notched gourd over which a bamboo 'brush', or a drumstick, is scraped.
guitar	Spanish string instrument. Has a large flat-backed body with *soundhole,* violin-like waisted shape, fretted neck and six strings, tuned E, A, D, G, B, E.
guitare d'amour	*Arpeggione.*
guitarra (P)	*Electric guitar.*
guitarra (Sp)	*Guitar* (classical).

78

guitarrón (Sp) — The *bass guitar* used in *mariachi* bands.

Gummischlegel (G) — Rubber stick.

gusla, gusle, or **guzla** — Ancient one-stringed bowed instrument popular in Bulgaria, Macedonia and Serbia.

gusli or **guslee** — Russian *zither*.

gusto (It) — Taste, style.

gut (G) — Good, well.

gymel — English term for the temporary splitting of one voice into two parts of equal range, used mainly in the fifteenth and sixteenth centuries.

gypsy scale — Hungarian minor scale: the *harmonic minor* with a raised fourth degree, popular in Hungarian Romantic music.

H

H (G)
: The note or key B. (B flat is called B in German.)

h
: 'Hammer-on' in guitar tablature.

habanera (Sp)
: A slow Cuban dance, named after Havana (Habana).The dotted rhythm is similar to that of the *tango*.

Hackbrett (G)
: Dulcimer. *Schlagzither*.

hahnebüchen (G)
: Coarse, heavy.

hairpins
: Slang for *crescendo* and *diminuendo* signs.

halb, halbe (G)
: Half.

Halbe or **Halbenote** (G)
: Half note, minim.

Halbe-Pause (G)
: Half rest, minim rest.

Halbetaktnote (G)
: Half note or minim.

Halbprinzipal (G)
: Half-diapason.

Halbsopran (G)
: *Mezzo soprano*.

Halbtenor (G)
: *Baritone*.

Halbton (G)
: Semitone.

half cadence
: Also known as *imperfect cadence* or *dominant cadence*. The movement from *tonic*, or other chord, to *dominant*.

half-close
: *Half cadence*.

half note
: A note one half the duration of a whole note. *Minim*.

Hälfte (G)
: Half.

hallen (G)
: To clang, resound.

Halt (G)
: Pause. Note that the word *Pause* (pause) is not used. See *fermata*.

halten (G)
: To hold, sustain.

hammer-on
: A guitar technique, involving swiftly sounding a note and quickly and percussively fingering a string to the next note above.

Hammond
: Hammond organ, an innovative electric organ, which introduced *drawbars* and *tone-wheels*, developed in the mid-30s in America.

Hand, Hände (G)
: Hand, hands.

Handelian cadence
: A form of *hemiola* characteristic of the cadences of George Frederick Handel.Three chords of two beats' duration in a 3/4 piece. The center chord sits across the bar line.

Hände weg (G)
: Hands off.

hand horn
: The natural *French horn*.

Handregistrierung (G)
: Manual piston, on organ.

Hardanger fiddle	('Hardingfele' in Norwegian.) Folk violin with sympathetic strings.
hard bop	One of the two predominant post-bop jazz styles of the 1950s (the other was *West Coast*).
hardi, hardiment (F)	Bold, boldly.
Harfe (G)	*Harp.*
Harmon	A type of metal mute for *brass* instruments, the idea of Patrick T. 'Paddy' Harmon. It consists of two parts: a hollow body, into which fits a sliding cylindrical stem with a small horn at the end. Used to achieve a range of effects, from the crying *wah-wah* effect of early dance bands through to the characteristic muted sound associated with Miles Davis.
harmonica	Mouth organ. A small wind instrument with free metal reeds, that are sounded by blowing or sucking. Mouth organs are built in several sizes, and may be *diatonic* or *chromatic*. The name harmonica has also been used for a set of tuned glass bowls or glasses, called a *glass harmonica*.
harmonic minor	A diatonic scale in which the half steps occur between the second and third, fifth and sixth, and the seventh and tonic. There are three semitones between the sixth and seventh degrees.
harmonic rhythm	The rhythmic pattern of the changes of harmony.
harmonics	**1.** The single pure constituents of a complex sound. **2.** Sound made on string instruments by touching the string lightly at certain points. **3.** High notes obtained on woodwind instruments by the use of complex and non-standard fingering.
harmonic series	A series of notes produced above (and including) a low fundamental note. On the piano the series may begin, in an upward direction, with C (below bass clef), C, G, middle C, E, G, B♭, C, D, etc. Not all of the notes are in tune, and not all can always be heard.
harmonie (F)	*Harmony.*
Harmonie (G)	*Harmony, wind band.*
harmonie, basse d' (F)	*Ophicleide.*
harmonie, cor d' (F)	*French horn*, without valves.
Harmoniemusik (G)	Band of wood, brass and percussion.
harmonie, trompette d' (F)	*Trumpet.*

harmonique (F)	Harmonic.
harmonische Töne (G)	*Harmonics.*
harmonium	A keyboard instrument, resembling a small organ, but with *free reeds*. These are blown by bellows pumped by the player's feet.
harmony	1. The study of *chords*.
	2. When pitches are in agreement.
harp	Plucked seven-octave string instrument, with triangular frame, strung vertically. The modern orchestral harp has seven pedals which modify the tuning. The slang description 'naked piano' captures the essence of the instrument. There are many simple versions, without the pedals, including Celtic harp, Welsh triple harp, and the *clàrsach*.
harpsichord	Keyboard instrument with mechanically plucked strings. Prominent from c.1550 to 1800. See *spinet, virginals*.
hart, harte (G)	Hard, major.
hastig (G)	Hasty, hurried, rushed.
haupt (G)	Head, principal, chief.
Hauptdirigent (G)	Principal conductor.
Hauptprobe (G)	Dress rehearsal, final rehearsal.
Hauptrolle (G)	Principal role or part, lead.
Hauptstimme (G)	Principal voice, principal part.
Hauptthema (G)	Principal theme of a composition.
Hauptwerk (G)	Great organ.
haut, haute (F)	High.
hautbois (F)	*Oboe.*
hautbois d'amour (F)	*Oboe d'amore.*
havanaise (F)	*Habanera.*
Hawaiian guitar	1. Horizontal *steel guitar*.
	2. *Ukulele.*
head	1. Theme.
	2. A membrane stretched over a *drum, banjo* or *tambourine*.
head arrangement	An *arrangement* for a jazz *combo* or *big band* that evolves collectively, performance by performance, with nothing ever written down. Some of the repertoire of the great *swing* bands, (e.g. those of Count Basie and Duke Ellington), was created in this way.
headbanger	A fan of *heavy metal* music, who indulges in rapid

	rotary motion of the head in time to the music, or - allegedly - who is driven to bang the head against hard surfaces (sometimes the speaker cabinets) during performances.
heavy metal	Highly amplified rock music, 'set against the bloodier edge of the sword and sorcery market' according to a contemporary commentator.
Heckelphone	Bass oboe, made by the German firm of Heckel.
heel	The end of a violin bow held by the player. Same as *nut, frog*.
heftig (G)	Violent, impetuous.
heiss (G)	Hot, ardent.
heiter (G)	Merry, clear.
Heldentenor (G)	Heroic tenor.
helicon	A circular *tuba*, built for *marching bands*.
hell (G)	Clear, bright.
Hellflöte (G)	Clear flute organ stop.
hemidemisemiquaver	Sixty-fourth note.
hemiola	In three-four time, successions of two-beat phrases, undermining the time signature.
Herabstrich (G)	'Here-down-stroke.' Down-bow.
Heraufstrich (G)	'Here-up-stroke.' Up-bow.
Herbstlied (G)	Autumn song.
Herdenglocken (G)	Herd bells. *Cow bells*.
hernach (G)	Hereafter.
héroïque (F), **heroisch** (G)	Heroic.
Herstrich (G)	'Hither-stroke'. Down stroke on cello and double bass.
Hertz	A unit of measurement of frequency, equivalent to one complete cycle per second.
herunterstimmen (G)	To tune down a string.
Herunterstrich (G)	Down-bow on violin and viola.
hervorgehoben (G)	'Forth-heaved.' A melody to be brought out.
hervorragend (G)	'Forth-projecting.' Prominent.
hervortretend (G)	To emerge, (to step out).
herzhaft, herzlich (G)	Hearty, warm, heartfelt.
herzig (G)	Tender, charming.
Hes (G)	B flat, though B flat is usually called B in German.
Heses (G)	B double flat.
heterophony	Simultaneous performance of two or more slightly different versions of the same melody.
hexachord	Six-note scale.

hier (G)	Here.
hi-fi, high fidelity	Obsolete term to describe good quality sound reproduction. Now used to describe domestic equipment as opposed to professional products.
high-hat (hi-hat)	A pair of cymbals mounted horizontally, face to face, the lower one is fixed, the upper one raised or lowered by a foot pedal.
Hilfsdirigent (G)	Assistant conductor.
Hilfslinie (G)	*Leger line.*
Hilfsorganist (G)	Assistant organist.
hinsterbend (G)	Dying away.
Hinstrich (G)	'Away stroke'. The up-bow on cello and double bass.
hinter der Bühne (G)	Backstage.
hip-hop	A mixture of a heavy *disco* beat, usually played on drum machines and synthesizers, with spoken rhymed lyrics that frequently refer to current issues or personalities. A strand in the development of *rap* music.
Hirt (G)	Herd.
His (G)	B sharp.
h.o.b.	Hand over bell. An instruction to brass players.
Hoboe (G)	*Oboe.*
Hoboken	Anthony van Hoboken (1887-1983), who compiled the catalog of the works of Haydn.
höchst (G)	Highest, most.
Hochzeitsmarsch (G)	Wedding march.
Hochzeitszug (G)	Wedding procession.
hocket, hoquet	An early contrapuntal effect where one melody was taken alternately by two voices, a rest in one voice coinciding with a note in the other, producing a hiccup effect.
hoedown	American folk dance.
Hofbühne (G)	'Court stage'. Court theater.
Hofkapelle (G)	Court chapel.
Hofoper (G)	Court opera, court opera house.
Hoforganist (G)	Court organist.
Hoftrompeter (G)	Court trumpeter.
Höhe (G)	Height.
Holz (G)	Wood.
Holzbläser (G)	'Wood-blowers', i.e. *woodwind* players.
Holzblasinstrumente (G)	'Wood-blow-instruments', i.e. *woodwind*.
Holzharmonika (G)	*Xylophone.*

Holzschlägel (G)	Wooden drumstick.
homophone	Two strings tuned to produce the same note.
homophonic, homophony	Music where the parts move together, where one part has the melody. The opposite of *polyphony*.
homorhythmic	Music in which all parts move in the same rhythm.
honky-tonk	1. A cheap, out-of-tune piano.
	2. A piano style, related to *boogie-woogie*.
	3. A bar or dive.
hook	A catchy *jingle* or theme.
hora	An Israeli circle dance, originating in Romania.
horn	Jazz slang for any wind instrument. Also *axe*.
Hörner (G)	Horns (orchestral).
hornpipe	Ancient solo dance of British origin.
horns (jazz)	Slang for any wind instruments. The *front line*.
hot jazz	Pre-war term for any up-tempo instrumental jazz performance.
house	Dance music that originated in Chicago, in the Warehouse club, hence the name. A descendant of *disco*, popular in the late 1980s.
howlback, howlround	*Feedback.*
hübsch (G)	Pretty, dainty.
humoresque (F), **Humoreske** (G)	General term for a good-humored composition.
hüpfend (G)	Hopping. Springing bow.
hurdy-gurdy	Mechanical stringed instrument played by turning a handle which rotates a rosined wheel. This wheel acts like a bow in vibrating the strings. Melody notes are changed by a key-operated mechanism.
hurtig (G)	Nimble, agile.
huruk	Hourglass-shaped Indian drum.
hydraulis	(From the Greek for 'water' and 'pipe'.) Greco-Roman forerunner of the modern pipe organ in which water was used to control the wind pressure.
hymn	The praise of God by singing.
Hz.	*Hertz.*

I

i (It) — The.

Ibérien, Ibérienne (F) — Spanish (also, strictly, Portuguese). Iberian.

idée fixe (F) — Fixed idea. Obsession.

il (It) — The.

il faut (F) — It is necessary to, one must.

imitation — In counterpoint, one voice repeating a figure previously stated by another voice.

immer (G) — Always.

impair (F) — Odd (numbers).

impaziente, impazientemente (It) — Impatient, impatiently.

imperfect cadence — Progression *tonic* to *dominant*.

imperioso (It) — Imperious.

impeto (It) — Impetus, impetuosity.

impétueux (F) — Impetuous.

impetuoso, impetuosamente (It) — Impetuous, impetuously.

imponente (It) — Imposing.

imponierend (G) — Imposing.

impresario — A promoter, agent or manager of events.

Impressionism — A description borrowed from painting. The Impressionists were so named after a painting by Monet, 'Sunrise; an Impression.' The painters Cézanne, Degas, Monet, Pissarro, Renoir and Sisley were all described as Impressionists. Debussy is characterized as the leading Impressionist of music. Others include Ravel, Dukas, Ibert and Delius.

impromptu — Unprompted. A short quasi-improvised piece.

improvisation — Spontaneous quasi-composition.

incalcando (It) — Getting faster and louder.

incalzando (It) — Getting quicker.

incidental music — Short pieces that accompany a play.

inciso (It) — Incisive.

incominciando (It) — Commencing.

indebolendo (It) — Becoming weak.

indeciso (It) — Undecided, capricious.

indicato (It) — Prominent.

indie — Independent record company.

infra (It) — Below.

inglese (It)	English.
in hat	Play into a hat *mute*.
in modo di (It)	In the manner of.
innig (G)	Heartfelt, sincere, intimately.
inno (It)	*Hymn.*
innocenza (It)	Innocence.
inquiet (F), **inquieto** (It)	Unquiet, restless.
in rilievo (It)	Prominent. Make the melody stand out.
insensibile (It)	Imperceptible.
insieme (It)	Together, ensemble.
Inspizient (G)	Stage manager.
Inspiziententisch (G)	Prompt desk.
inständig (G)	Urgent.
instante (It)	Urgent.
intavolatura (It)	Scoring.
Intendant (G)	Manager.
interlude	1. *Episode* in a *fugue*.
	2. General term for music between the main parts of a work.
intermedio,	'In the middle'. An instrumental *interlude*
intermezzo (It),	during the course of a ballet, opera or play.
intermède (F)	
Interpret (G)	Interpreter - performer or conductor.
interrupted cadence	A progression from the *dominant* to any chord other than the *tonic*. Often the *submediant*, chord VI.
interval	The difference in pitch between any two notes.
intime (F), **intimo** (It)	Intimate.
intonation	1. The act of singing or playing in tune.
	2. The opening phrase of a *plainsong* melody.
intrada	Preliminary piece.
intrepido,	Bold, boldness.
intrepidezza (It)	
intro	*Introduction.*
introduction	Preparatory music.
introduzione (It)	*Introduction.*
Introit	Entrance. *Psalm* sung at the beginning of the Roman Catholic *Mass*.
inversion of chords	A chord whose bass is a note other than the root.
inversion of intervals	Transferring the lower note of an interval an octave higher, or vice versa. An interval and its inversion always add up to nine. Thus a second becomes a seventh; two and seven add up to nine.

inverted pedal	A pedal point on any note other than the bass.
inverted turn	Begins with the lower auxiliary note, instead of the upper one.
Ionian	Medieval *mode* on C, whose note pattern is the same as the major scale.
IPS	Inches Per Second. Tape speed.
ira (It)	Ire, wrath.
IRCAM	Institut de Recherche et de Coordination Acoustique/Musique. A Paris-based experimental institute founded by Pierre Boulez in 1976, alongside its resident orchestra, the Ensemble InterContemporain.
Irish harp	Small harp without pedals.
ironico, ironicamente (It)	Ironic, ironically.
irresoluto (It)	Irresolute.
islancio, con (It)	Impetuously.
ISM	Incorporated Society of Musicians.
isorhythmic	Of equal rhythm. A phrase or melody where the pitch is varied but the rhythmic pattern is repeated.
istesso (It)	The same.
istesso tempo, l' (It)	'The same time'. The beat remains the same.
istrumento d'acciaio	'Instrument of steel'. Mozart's name for the *glockenspiel* in The Magic Flute.
Italian sixth	Type of augmented sixth chord, with the notes, in the key of C on the flattened *supertonic* (minor second of the scale), reading upwards, D♭, F, B. See *French sixth*, *German sixth*.

J

jabo (Sp)	A slow solo Spanish dance.
jácara (Sp)	Old Spanish song-dance.
jack	1. Component of the mechanism of a *harpsichord*.
	2. Electrical socket into which electronic devices (headphones, microphones, amplifiers) are plugged.
jackplug	Cable-mounted connector, which fits into a jack socket.
Jagdhorn (G)	Hunting horn.
Jäger (G)	Hunter.
jaleo	A slow solo Spanish dance.
Jalousieschweller (G)	Venetian blind swell. Organ swell pedal mechanism.
jam, jam session, jamming	An impromptu get-together of (originally) jazz or rock musicians, where simple themes or standards are played and improvised on.
jammernd, jämmerlich (G)	Lamenting, lamentable.
Jannisary music (Eng), **Janitscharenmusik** (G)	Turkish type of military band music. The Jannisaries were the Sultan's bodyguard, disbanded 1826.
jarabe	Type of Mexican popular dance.
jaw's harp	*Jew's harp.*
jazz	Music that began in North America at the end of the nineteenth century, and was first heard on record (by the Original Dixieland Jazz Band, (ODJB) from New Orleans) in 1917. Early bands had a *front line* of trumpet (or cornet), clarinet and trombone, and sometimes saxophone. Initially the *rhythm section* often contained double bass (less frequently wind bass) and drum kit, sometimes guitar or piano and later, for a period, banjo. The drum kit is one of the innovations that jazz gave to popular music. See *swing, bebop, hard bop, cool, acid jazz* and *free jazz*.
je (G)	Always, ever, each.
jedoch (G)	Still, nevertheless, yet.
jeté (F)	Flung. Bouncing the bow on the string on the down-bow.
jeu, jeux (F)	Play. Games.
jeu ordinaire (F)	An instruction to play normally after an instruction to play in an unusual way.

jew's harp	A small open-ended circular metal frame, surrounding a strip of spring steel fastened at one end. The frame is gripped between the teeth, and the steel strip twanged with the fingers. Also called in German *Judenharfe, Maultrommel, Brummeisen* and *Mundharmonika*. In French it is called *guimbarde, trompe de Béarn,* and *trompe de laquais.* In Italian, *scacciapensieri, spassapensieri* and *aura.*
jig	A lively leaping folk dance.
jingle	1. Music composed for a commercial. 2. Circular metal plates fitted to a tambourine.
jingling Johnny	Instrument shaped like a small tree, hung with bells and shaken. Also called *Chinese pavilion,* or *Turkish crescent.*
jive	1. Type of free dancing associated with jazz during the 1930s, and later with *rock 'n' roll* in the 1950s. 2. Boastful, exaggerated talk.
joik, joiking	Traditional unaccompanied singing of the Smi people (Laplanders), from the north of Norway, Sweden, Finland and Russia. Was supresssed in the nineteenth century.
jongo (P)	Rural samba from southeastern Brazil.
joropa	A Latin dance in fast 3/4 time.
jota	Northern Spanish dance in fast 3/4 time.
jouer (F)	To play.
joyeux, joyeuse (F)	Joyful.
jubelnd (G)	Jubilant.
Jubilate	Latin name for Psalm 100, 'O be joyful in the Lord'.
jubiloso (Sp)	Jubilant.
Judenharfe (G)	*Jew's harp.*
jug band	A folk band of varying instrumentation, but using one or more narrow-necked jugs sounded by blowing across the opening.
juke box	A record player, coin operated. In the Southern United States, 'juke' is the name for an inn.
jungle music	A term used to describe the Cotton Club period (1925-1930) of Duke Ellington. His orchestration made use of *plunger mutes, growl* effects and high clarinets.
jusqu' à (F)	Until.

juste (F)
just intonation

Just.
System of tuning in which all intervals are pure rather than tempered. See *temperament*.

K

K

1. Abbreviation for Köchel. Ludwig von Köchel (1800-1877) compiled the catalog of Mozart's works, and Köchel numbers (e.g. K 85) now identify them. **2.** Abbreviation for Kirkpatrick. Ralph Kirkpatrick (1911-1984) compiled the catalog of Domenico Scarlatti's works.

kalimba
African thumb piano. *Mbira*.

kamancha
Instrument to accompany Ashough (Armenian troubadour) songs. See also *duduk, kanon, tar*.

Kammer (G)
Chamber.

Kammerkonzert (G)
Chamber concert.

Kammermusik (G)
Chamber music.

Kammermusikvereinigung (G)
Chamber music ensemble.

Kammerorchester (G)
Chamber orchestra.

Kammersänger (G)
Honorary title for a distinguished singer.

Kammerton (G)
Concert pitch.

Kammervirtuose (G)
Honorary title for a distinguished instrumentalist.

Kanon (G)
Canon.

kanon
Instrument used to accompany Ashough songs. See also *duduk, kamancha, tar*.

Kantate (G)
Cantata.

Kantor (G)
Church choirmaster.

Kantorei (G)
Church choral ensemble.

Kapelle (G)
1. Band, orchestra. **2.** Chapel.

Kapellmeister (G)
Master of the Chapel, director of music.

karaoke (Japanese)
'Empty orchestra'. Amateur singing with recorded backing.

Kastagnetten (G)
Castanets.

kaum (G)
Barely, hardly.

kazoo
A conical metal instrument, played by humming, with a paper membrane fitted as a sound coloring device.

keck (G)
Audacious, bold, pert.

keineswegs (G)
In no way.

Kesselpauke (G)
Kettledrum.

kettledrum
Timpani. Cupola-shaped drum, which rests on a stand with the single skin facing upwards. The tension of the head can be varied to change the pitch.

key	1. Tonal center. 2. The lever on an instrument, depressed to produce a note.
keyboard	The arrangement of keys, e.g. on a piano, organ or synthesizer, to be played by fingers or feet.
keyboard lab	A room containing many slave keyboards, equipped with headphones, all linked to a master keyboard. Used in educational establishments to give cheap (and inferior) piano lessons.
keyed bugle	*Ophicleide.*
keynote	*Tonic.*
key signature	The group of *sharps* or *flats* in written music, indicating the key.
kicks	Accents in jazz, usually supplied by the drummer.
Kielflügel (G)	*Harpsichord.*
kin	A small *koto*. Ancient seven-string *zither* originating in China.
Kind, Kinder (G)	Child, children.
Kinderstück (G)	Children's piece.
kindlich (G)	Childlike.
Kinnstütze (G)	Chin rest.
Kirche (G)	Church.
Kissentanz (G)	*Cushion dance.*
kit	1. Tiny pocket-violin once used by dancing masters. 2. Kit percussion, meaning the kit used by jazz or rock players.
kithara	Ancient Greek *lyre.*
Klage (G)	Lament.
klagend, kläglich (G)	Lamenting.
Klang (G)	Sound, tone, tonal quality, timbre.
Klangfarbenmelodie (G)	'Tone-color melody', in which notes or scraps of melody are passed between voices. Term proposed by Schoenberg.
klanglich (G)	Sonorously.
klangvoll (G)	Sonorous.
Klappe (G)	Key of a wind instrument.
Klappenhorn (G)	Keyed *bugle.*
Klappentrompete (G)	Valve *trumpet.*
klar (G)	Clear, distinct.
Klarinette, **Klarinetten** (G)	*Clarinet*, clarinets.
Klaviatur (G)	*Keyboard.*
Klavichord (G)	*Clavichord.*

Klavier (G)	1. Any stringed keyboard instrument.
	2. *Piano.*
Klavierauszug (G)	*Piano score*, piano arrangement.
Klavierhauptprobe (G)	Piano technical rehearsal.
Klavierspiel (G)	Piano playing.
Klavierspieler (G)	Pianist, piano player.
Klavierstimmer (G)	Piano tuner.
Klavierunterricht (G)	Piano lessons, piano instruction.
klein (G)	Small, minor.
kleine Terz (G)	Minor third.
kleine Trommel (G)	*Side drum, snare drum.*
Klezmer	Instrumental and vocal music in the Yiddish musical tradition, originally used for weddings and special occasions, and taken to America at the end of the nineteenth century during the large scale emigration of Jews from Eastern Europe.
Klezmorim (Yiddish)	Plural of *Klezmer*. Also **Klesmorim**.
klingen (G)	To sound.
Knabenchor (G)	Boys' choir.
Knarre (G)	Rattle.
kneifend (G)	Plucking, *pizzicato*.
Knollhorn (G)	Herald horn.
kokett (G)	Coquettish.
kolomyika	Polish dance.
Kolophon (G)	Bow rosin. *Colophony* (resin acid, predominantly abietic acid) named after Colophon, or Kolophon, in the Izmir region of Ionia.
Kombination (G)	Combination.
komisch (G)	Comic.
komponieren (G)	To compose.
Komponist (G)	Composer.
Kompositionsstunde (G)	Composition class.
konsequent (G)	Strict, rigorous.
Konservatorium (G)	*Conservatory.*
Kontrabaß (G)	Double bass.
Kontrafagott (G)	Double bassoon.
Kontrapunkt (G)	*Counterpoint.*
Konzert (G)	1. Concert.
	2. *Concerto.*
Konzertmeister (G)	*Leader* of an orchestra.
Kopist (G)	*Copyist.*
kora	Plucked string instrument from West Africa.
Korean temple block	*Temple block.*

Kornett (G)	*Cornet.*
Korrepetitor (G)	*Répétiteur.*
Kostüm (G)	Costume.
Kostümbildner (G)	Costume designer.
koto	Japanese string instrument, a long *zither* with thirteen silk strings stretched over movable bridges. See *kin.*
Kraft (G)	Strength.
kräftig (G)	Strong.
Krakowiak	Polish dance in fast 2/4 time, from Cracow region.
Krebs (G)	*Retrograde* (in serialism).
Krebsgang (G)	Any composition which is as effective backwards as forwards.
Kreis (G)	Circle. Cycle.
Kreuz (G)	*Sharp* sign. Cross.
Krieg (G)	War.
Krumhorn,	*Crumhorn.* A family of medieval wind
Krummhorn (G)	instruments, with *double reed* and J-shaped body.
Krummbogen (G)	*Crook* of a brass instrument.
Kuhglocke (G)	*Cowbell.*
Kulissen (G)	Scenery. (Theater).
Kunst (G)	Art.
Kunstkopf (G)	*Dummy head,* used in stereo recording.
Künstler (G)	Artist.
Künstlergarderobe (G)	Dressing-room.
Kunstlied (G)	Art-song.
Kunstwerk (G)	Work of art.
kurz, kurzer (G)	Short, shorter.
Kyrie (Greek)	Lord Have Mercy (Kyrie Eleison). The only part of the *Mass* which is sung in Greek.

L

la	Sixth note of the diatonic scale. Spelt 'lah' in *tonic sol-fa.*
Labialstimme (G)	Flue stop.
lächelnd (G)	Smiling.
lâcher (F)	To loosen.
lacrimoso (It), **lagrimoso** (Sp)	Sad, tearful.
Lage (G)	Position.
lagnoso, lagnevole (It)	Doleful.
laid back	Nonchalant, unfussed, carefree, *cool.*
Laie (G)	Amateur.
laisser (F)	To allow, to leave.
laissez vibrer (F)	Let vibrate, let sound.
lambada	Dance, originating from Brazil. A fusion of *merengue* and carimbó. Briefly popular worldwide in the early 1990s.
lament	A mournful piece. To be played at a funeral or the commemoration of a death.
lamentando, lamentoso (It)	Lamenting. Mournful.
Lampenfieber (G)	Butterflies, stage fright.
lancio (It)	Gusto.
Landini cadence	The melodic line of the leading note, the sixth degree and the tonic, *ti-la-do*, frequently used by the fourteenth century Italian composer Francesco Landini.
Ländler (G)	An Austrian dance, similar to the *waltz,* but slower.
ländlich (G)	Country-like, rural, rustic.
lang (G)	Long, lengthy.
langoureux, langoureusement (F)	Languorous, languorously.
langsam (G)	Slow.
langsamer (G)	Slower.
languendo, languente, languemente (It)	Languishing.
langueur (F)	Languor.
languido, languidamente (It)	Languid, languidly.
languissant (F)	Languishing.
languore (It)	Languor.

lap piano	Slang term coined by the American guitarist George Van Eps for his innovative seven-string guitar.
lap steel guitar	An amplified *steel guitar* that is held horizontally, in the lap or on a table.
largamente (It)	Broadly.
large (F)	Broad. Slow, dignified.
largement (F)	Broadly.
largeur (F)	Breadth.
larghetto (It)	Rather slow.
larghezza (It)	Breadth.
largo (It)	Slow, stately.
lasciare (It)	To allow to.
lassen (G)	To leave.
Last Post	An army bugle call, traditionally played at 10:00 p.m. to signal the end of the day. Also played at military funerals and, since 1918, every evening at the Menin Gate Memorial at Ypres.
Latin American	The music and instruments of Central and South America.
laud (Sp)	*Lute.*
laut (G)	Loud.
Laut (G)	Sound.
Laute (G)	*Lute.*
läuten (G)	To chime, ring.
Lautenist (G)	Lutenist.
Lautenmacher (G)	*Luthier.* Maker of string instruments.
Lautstärke (G)	*Dynamic.*
layering	In *synthesis*; multiple voices combined to sound together when a note is played.
LCD	Liquid Crystal Display. Produces dark symbols against a light background.
lead	To play the principal part.
leader	**1.** Concert master, principal first violin. See *chef d'attaque*. The conductor or bandleader is sometimes also called leader, particularly in America. **2.** Colored plastic tape fixed to the end of a recording tape, for identification and protection.
leading note	Seventh degree of the diatonic scale.
lead sheet	A simplified, but complete, version of a song, giving *top line*, *lyrics* and *chord symbols*.
leap	An interval larger than one letter-name or one step. More than a second.

lebendig (G)	Lively.
lebhaft (G)	Lively (like *vivace*).
LED	Light Emitting Diode. A semiconductor diode, used for displays on musical equipment. Produces light symbols against a dark background.
ledger lines, leger lines	Short lines written above or below the *staff*.
leer (G)	Empty.
leere Saite (G)	*Open string.*
legato (It)	Smooth.
legatura (It)	Tie, slur. Also *syncopation*.
légèrement (F), **leggiero** (It)	Light.
leggiadro, leggiadretto (It)	Graceful.
leggio (It)	Music desk.
legno (It)	Wood.
leicht (G)	Light, lightweight. Also easy, simple.
leichtfertig (G)	Giddy, frivolous.
Leichtigkeit (G)	Lightness. Also ease.
Leid (G)	Grief, pain, sorrow.
Leidenschaft (G)	Passion.
leidenschaftlich (G)	Passionate.
Leierkasten (G)	*Barrel organ.*
leise (G)	Quiet, soft, gentle.
leisten (G)	To perform.
Leistung (G)	Performance.
leiten (G)	To direct, to conduct.
Leiter (G)	Director, conductor.
leitmotif (Eng), **Leitmotiv** (G)	Leading theme. A theme associated with a specific character or event in opera, film and TV music.
Leitton (G)	*Leading note.*
Leitung (G)	Direction.
lene, leno (It)	Faint. Gentle.
Lent	The forty days (not counting Sundays) between Ash Wednesday and Easter.
lent (F), **lento** (It)	Slow.
Leslie speaker, Leslie cabinet	A speaker developed in 1940 by Don Leslie for use with the *Hammond* organ. The speaker colors the sound by rotating.
lesto (It)	Quick. Lively.
letzt (G)	Last.
levare (It)	To lift, or take off.
levezza (It)	Lightness.

98

LFO	Low Frequency Oscillator.
L.H.	Left Hand. Instruction for keyboard players.
liberamente (It)	Freely.
libertà (It)	Liberty, freedom.
libitum (L)	See *ad libitum*.
libre, librement (F)	Free, freely.
libretto (It)	Little book. The text of an opera or musical.
licenza (It)	License, freedom.
lick	Short melodic musical phrase.
licorice stick	Obsolete slang for clarinet.
lié (F)	Bound. Slurred or tied. Smoothly, *legato*.
Liebe (G)	Love.
Liebesgeige (G)	*Viola d'amore.*
Liebesoboe (G)	*Oboe d'amore.*
lieblich (G)	Lovely.
Lied, Lieder (G)	Song, songs.
Liederkreis (G)	Song cycle.
Lied ohne Worte (G)	Song without words.
lieto (It)	Joyful.
lieve (It)	Light, easy.
ligado (Sp)	A guitar slurring technique, where notes are played with the left hand alone.
ligature	**1.** In *single reed instruments*, the device that secures the reed to the mouthpiece. **2.** A slur or tie over a group of notes, denoting that they are to be sung to the same syllable.
limiter	A *signal* processor that limits. (Performs *limiting*).
limiting	The electronic control that keeps an *audio* signal from exceeding a certain level.
Liniensystem (G)	*Stave.*
linke Hand (G)	Left hand.
links (G)	Left. Stage left (prompt side).
lip	*Embouchure.*
lip trill	A *trill* on a brass instrument, done with the *embouchure.*
lirico (It)	*Lyric.*
liscio (It)	Smooth.
l'istesso (It)	The same.
liuto (It)	*Lute.*
livre (F)	Book.
loben (G)	To praise.
locked hands	See *block chords.*
loco (It)	Place. At the normal pitch.

Locrian	A medieval *mode*, as though starting on the seventh degree of the diatonic major scale. Thus the semitones are between the first and second steps and between the fourth and fifth steps.
Loge (G)	Theater box.
lointain (F), **lontano** (It)	Distant.
looping, loops	**1.** In *synthesis*, the repetition of a musical phrase or piece of a sample. **2.** On film tracks, the repetitive use of background sound effects, such as street noise or conversation.
los (G)	Loose, free in style.
los! (G)	Go!
louden, louden lots	*Crescendo*, term coined by Percy Grainger (1882-1961), Australian pianist, composer and collector of folk songs.
lourd (F)	Heavy.
loure (F)	**1.** A French *bagpipe*. **2.** A dance with *bagpipe* accompaniment.
louré (F)	*Legato* bowing.
LP	Long Player. A vinyl record used for domestic sound reproduction. Current between late 1950s and late 1980s, when the *CD* began to replace it.
luftig (G)	Airy. Light.
Luftpause (G)	A pause for breath.
lugubre (It)	Mournful.
lullaby	Cradle song.
lumineux (F)	Luminous.
lungo, lunga (It)	Long.
lusingando (It)	Coaxing. Persuasive.
lustig (G)	Cheerful, merry.
Lustspiel Komödie	Comic opera.
lute	Fretted stringed instrument, plucked with the fingers. Characterized by large bulbous 'pear shaped' body with flat belly, strings tuned in pairs, and an angled *pegbox*.
luth (F)	*Lute.*
lutherie	*Lute* making. The phrase is extended to mean the making of *guitars* and members of the violin family.
luthier	Lute maker. Maker of stringed instruments.
lutto (It)	Mourning.
l.v.	*Laissez vibrer.*

Lydian	The *mode* having scale steps equivalent to playing F to F in the key of C.
lyra, lyre	Plucked stringed instrument, like a small harp.
lyric	**1.** The words to a song.
	2. A term borrowed from poetry and applied to mean intermediate between light and dramatic, in describing voices (*'lyric soprano'*) or pieces of music ('lyric pieces').
lyric soprano	A female singer between a *coloratura* and a *dramatic soprano*.
lyric tenor	A male singer with a light flexible *tenor* range.
lyrique (F), **lyrisch** (G)	Lyrical.

M

ma (It) But.

macchina (It) Machine, mechanism.

machete Four-string folk guitar from Portugal.

machicotage (F) Ornamentation of solo parts in *plainsong*.

machine à vent (F) *Wind machine.*

mächtig (G) Mighty, powerful.

madrigal *Renaissance* secular vocal music, usually unaccompanied.

madrileña (Sp), Spanish dance from Madrid.
madrilène (F)

maestà, maestade (It) Majesty, dignity.

maestoso (It) Majestic.

maestrale (It) Masterly.

maestro (It) Master, teacher, conductor.

maggiolata (It) May song. Spring song.

maggiore (It) *Major.*

maggot An imprecise term, usually meaning country dance.

magno, magna (It) Great.

mailloche (F) Stick of bass drum.

main (F) Hand.

main droite (F) Right hand.

main gauche (F) Left hand.

mainstream Music in the current trend, or the middle-of-the-road from the recent past.

mais (F) But.

maître (F) Master.

maîtrise (F) Choir school.

majestätisch (G) Majestic.

majestueux, Majestic.
majestueuse (F)

majeur (F) *Major.*

major Greater. Used to describe chords, intervals and scales.

major chord A triad comprised of *root*, major third and perfect fifth.

major scale Two *tetrachords* of tone, tone, semitone, one placed a tone above the other. Thus, C, D, E, F. Then G, A, B, C. That is, the half steps occur between the third and fourth, and seventh and eighth degrees.

malagueña	Andalusian folk dance, from Málaga.
malinconico (It)	Melancholy.
malizia (It)	Malice.
mallet	A percussion beater, usually with a spherical head.
mambo	An Afro-Cuban dance popular in the 1940s.
mancando, mancante (It)	Dying away, fading away.
mancanza (It)	Lack.
mandocello	Bass *mandolin*.
mandola, mandora	Tenor *mandolin*.
mandolin, mandoline	Fretted instrument of the *lute* family, with eight strings tuned in pairs, and played with a *plectrum*.
manica (It)	Shift, on violin.
manico (It)	*Fingerboard*.
Manieren (G)	Ornaments, graces.
Männer (G)	Men.
Mannheim School	A group of mid-eighteenth century composers, headed by W. Stamitz, working at the court of Mannheim in Germany.
mano (It)	Hand.
mano destra (It)	Right hand.
mano sinistra (It)	Left hand.
manual	**1.** Organ or harpsichord keyboard. **2.** Instruction pamphlet to accompany electronic equipment.
manuscript, manuscript paper	Lined paper on which music is written.
maraca	Latin-American percussion instrument. A hollow container fitted with a handle. Originally a gourd filled with seeds. For greater volume the seeds were replaced by lead shot.
maracuta (P)	Slow, heavy Afro-Brazilian processional music.
marcando, marcato, marc. (It)	Emphatic, accented.
march	Music for marching, in 2/4 or 4/4 time.
marche (F)	*March*.
Märchen (G)	Tale, fairytale.
marching band	A band consisting of woodwind, brass and percussion that performs while marching. Also known as *military band*, *wind band* or (when not marching), a *concert band* or even symphonic wind band.
marcia (It)	*March*.
mardakion	A type of *accordion*.

Mardi Gras	Short for 'Mardi Gras Carnivale': 'On Tuesday we say goodbye to fat meat'. Shrove Tuesday. Same as *Carnaval*.
mariachi	Mexican folk band, usually two violins, guitar and *guitarrón*, a type of bass guitar.
marimba	A tuned percussion instrument, like a *xylophone*, but at lower pitch and with resonators.
markiert (G)	Marked.
markig (G)	Vigorous.
mark tree	A percussion instrument, with small brass tubes of varied lengths hung close together to give a shimmering, tinkling effect of indeterminate pitch when stroked.
marqué (F)	Marked, accented.
Marsch (G)	*March.*
marteau (F)	Hammer.
martelé (F), **martellato** (It)	Hammered. Strongly accented.
marziale (It)	In a military style.
mascarade (F)	*Masque*. Masquerade.
Maschinenpauken (G)	Mechanically tuned *kettledrums*.
masculine cadence	A *cadence* which resolves onto a strong beat.
Maskenbildner (G)	Make-up man.
masque, mask	A sixteenth century ceremonial social entertainment of the aristocracy, staged with music, singing, dancing, poetry and scenery.
Mass	Principal service of the Roman Catholic Church.
mäßig, (mässig) (G)	Moderate, moderately.
massimo, massima (It)	The greatest.
master	The version of a complete recording from which copies are duplicated.
master class	A public tutorial given by an expert.
master tape	The final mix of a recording from which *CDs* and *cassettes* will be made.
matelotte (F)	Sailor's *hornpipe*.
Matins	Mornings. The daily morning service.
mattinata (It)	Morning song.
Maultrommel (G)	*Jew's harp.*
mauresco (Sp), **mauresque** (F)	Moorish.
mazurka	A Polish dance in triple time.
mbira	*Thumb piano.*
MCPS	Mechanical Copyright Protection Society.

m. d.	*Main droite, mano destra*. Right hand.
mean-tone tuning	Tuning (usually of keyboard instruments until the early nineteeth century), using a scale somewhere between natural tuning and *equal temperament* tuning. In this system 'remote keys' were so far out that they could not be used.
measure	Bar. The space between two bar lines.
medesimo (It)	The same.
mediant	The third degree of the scale.
medley	A group of tunes linked together.
megaphone	A conical tube open at both ends, used to direct and focus the voice. *Speaking trumpet*. Used by dance band singers before amplification, and famously in Walton's Façade (1920s). Electronic versions (loud-hailers) were produced in the later decades of the twentieth century.
mehr (G)	More.
mehrere (G)	Several.
Meister (G)	Master.
melisma	Several notes sung to one syllable.
mellophone	A brass bass instrument, constructed for marching. Some have been made from fiberglass.
melodeon	A type of small *concertina*, with free reeds, bellows, and keys.
melodica	Free reed wind instrument, mouth blown, with a keyboard.
melodic minor	A scale that differs in its ascending and descending forms. It has semitones between steps 2-3 and 7-8 ascending, and between steps 6-5 and 3-2 descending.
même (F)	Same.
meno (It)	Less.
menuet (F)	*Minuet.*
merengue	Caribbean song and dance in 2/4 time, originally from the Dominican Republic. Popular in the 1950s as a ballroom dance in the USA.
messa di voce (It)	Placing of the voice. *Crescendo* and *diminuendo* on a long-held note.
Messing (G)	Brass.
mesto (It)	Sad.
metà (It)	Half.
metallophone	Tuned percussion instrument, similar to the *xylophone* but with metal bars instead of wood.

meter, metre	Meter is concerned with the basic unvarying pulse of the music, as opposed to rhythm, which is concerned with the time-patterns of the notes within that meter. Thus 11/8 and 3/4 are different kinds of meters.
metronome	A small device for sounding or showing the number of beats per minute. Patented in 1815 by J. N. Maelzel, it was originally a clockwork mechanism controlled by an inverted variable length pendulum. This type has now been replaced by various electrical and electronic types, and even a version in the form of a tape measure, with the tape container serving as the pendulum weight.
mettere (It), **mettre** (F)	To put.
mezzo, mezza (It)	Half.
mezzo soprano	Female voice between *soprano* and *alto*.
mf	Abbreviation of 'mezzo forte', half loud.
m.g.	*Main gauche*. French for 'left hand'.
mi	The third degree of the *diatonic* scale.
microtonal, microtone	Small intervals not part of the *twelve-tone equal temperament* system.
middle C	C=256 Hz, in the middle of the *grand staff,* and approximately in the middle of the piano keyboard.
middle eight	*Release, bridge.*
middle-fiddle	*Viola,* term coined by Percy Grainger (1882-1961).
MIDI	Musical Instrument Digital Interface. A means by which electronic instruments can share digital information.
MIDI channel	The *pathway* along which *MIDI* information travels.
MIDI ports	Receptacles for cables.
milieu (F)	Middle.
militaire (F), **militare** (It), **Militär** (G)	Military.
Militärkapelle (G)	*Military band.*
Militärtrommel (G)	*Side drum.*
military band	*Marching band, wind band.* A term originally applied to regimental bands.
minaccevole, minaccevolmente (It)	Menacing, menacingly.
minder (G)	Less.

mineur (F)	*Minor.*
miniature score	A complete score published in as small a size as is practical. Used for study or, sometimes, for attending concerts.
MiniDisc	An erasable optical disc, similar to a *CD*, but half the size.
minim	British term for *half note*.
minimalism	A late twentieth century musical style employing simple music materials, much repetition and slow or no variation. The word is borrowed from a major art movement of the 1960s. Exponents include John Adams, Philip Glass, Steve Reich and Terry Riley.
Minne (G)	Courtly love, worship or adoration of a woman (often unattainable) by a knight or *troubadour* in the twelfth to fourteenth centuries.
Minnelied (G)	Love song.
Minnesinger (G)	*Troubadour.*
minor	Lesser.
minor chord	Chord containing a root, minor third and perfect fifth.
minor scale	See *melodic minor, harmonic minor, natural minor.*
minstrel	Medieval musical performer.
minuet	A French dance in moderate 3/4 time. Usually the third movement in *sonatas* and *symphonies* of the *classical* period.
min'yo	Generic name for a range of Japanese songs for work, dance, weddings and drinking.
mirliton (F)	*Kazoo.*
Missa (L)	*Mass.*
misterioso (It)	Mysterious.
mistero (It)	Mystery.
mistico (It)	Mystic.
misura (It)	Measure. Time.
mit (G)	With.
Mitte (G)	Middle.
mix	The processing - combining and *balancing* - of tracks of a recording.
mixer	1. The console which is used for mixing. 2. The operative performing the mixing.
Mixolydian	A medieval *mode* with the scale steps equivalent to playing G to G in the key of C major.

MM	Metronome Mark, or Maeltzel's Metronome.
moda (P)	Sentimental song from Portugal.
moda de violão (P)	Rural Brazilian folk song, often performed by two guitarist-vocalists singing in thirds.
modal	Pertaining to *modes*.
mode	A way of arranging the notes of a scale.
moderato (It), **modéré** (F)	At a moderate speed.
modern	Generally applied to music of the twentieth century onwards.
modern jazz	Specifically applied to the post-war New York based *bebop* movement which grew up around 52nd Street, associated with Charlie Parker, Dizzy Gillespie, Thelonious Monk and others.
modinha (P)	Style of sentimental Brazilian song.
modo (It)	**1.** Manner. **2.** *Mode.*
modulate, modulation	**1.** To change keys. **2.** In *synthesis*, using the level of an output to control the operation of a function.
möglich (G)	Possible.
moins (F)	Less.
moitié (F)	Half.
Moll (G)	*Minor.*
molle, mollemente (It)	Gentle, gently.
Mollton (G)	Minor note, i.e. note characterizing a minor scale.
molto (It)	Much, very much.
mono, monophonic, monophony	**1.** Music with a single line melody only. With no support or accompaniment. **2.** Single channel sound - as opposed to *stereo*.
monochord	A soundbox with a single string, calibrated accurately so that fundamental string ratios and acoustic principles can be determined and demonstrated. More a scientific instrument than a musical one.
monody	Solo (or *unison*) song with accompaniment. Melody and *continuo*.
monotone	Single unvaried pitch.
monter (F)	To raise.
Moog synthesizer	Electronic musical instrument invented by American engineer R. A. Moog in the late 1960s.
MOR	Middle-Of-the-Road. A music marketing term for *easy listening* music.

morceau (F)	Piece.
mordent	An ornament where the written note is either: (a) followed by a note immediately below, followed by the original note (**lower mordent**), or: (b) followed by a note immediately above, followed by the original note (**upper mordent**).
morendo (It)	Dying away.
Morgenlied (G)	Morning song.
mosso (It)	With motion, animated.
motet	A choral composition, usually on a sacred text.
motif (Eng.) (F), **Motiv** (G), **motivo** (It)	A short recurrent musical phrase.
moto, movimento (It)	Movement, motion.
moto perpetuo (It)	Perpetual motion, *perpetuum mobile*.
Motown	From '**Mo**tor **Town**', Detroit, the town in which The Motown Record Corporation is based. Music of the musicians of the 60s and 70s associated with that record label.
mouth harp	**1.** *Jew's harp*. **2.** *Harmonica*.
mouth organ	*Harmonica*.
mouthpiece	On brass and woodwind instruments, the part in contact with the player's lips.
mouvement, mouvt. (F)	Movement, motion.
mouvementé (F)	Animated.
movable doh	A system of singing, using syllables that relate to particular degrees of the scale. Each note is thus relative to the others, and not absolute in terms of a fixed pitch reference.
movement	A self-contained section or division of a large musical composition.
mp	'Mezzo piano' (It), half soft.
m.s.	*Mano sinistra* (It), left hand.
multi timbral	In *synthesis*, the capability to play simultaneously more than one tone color.
multitracking	Recording each voice or instrument on a separate track. A tape recorder with more than two tracks.
Mundharmonika (G)	Mouth harmonica, *mouth organ*.
Mundstück (G)	*Mouthpiece.*
munter (G)	Lively, cheerful.
murmelnd (G), **murmurando** (It)	Murmuring.
musetta (It), **musette** (F)	**1.** An early French *bagpipe*. **2.** A dance having a drone bass accompaniment.

3. A tonal quality on the *accordion*, obtained by tuning.

musica ficta (L) Feigned music. Practice, current for three centuries from c. 1350, where performers added *accidentals* to certain notes - e.g. those of the *tritone* - because they were deemed objectionable.

musical box, music box A small mechanical (usually clockwork) device in which a melody is played on the tuned metal teeth of a 'comb', which are plucked by pins mounted on a rotating drum.

musical glasses *Glass harmonica.*

musical saw A flexible carpenter's saw. Held between the knees, it is bowed with a violin bow or beaten with a mallet to produce a sound. The pitch is varied by bending the saw.

music center Domestic stereo system, often in a single box.

music drama Term used by Richard Wagner (1813-1883) to describe his operas after Lohengrin, when music, drama and staging are equally important.

musicology Musical scholarship.

music therapy The use of music as part of medical or psychological treatment.

Musikant (G) *Minstrel.*

Musiker (G) Musician.

Musikerziehung (G) Music education.

Musikfest (G) Music festival.

Musikgeschäft (G) Music shop.

Musikhochschule (G) Music college.

Musiklehre (G) Music theory.

Musiksendung (G) Music broadcast.

Musikstunde (G) Music lesson.

Musikverlag (G) Music publishing house.

Musikwissenschaft (G) Musicology.

musique concrète (F) Concrete music. Organization on tape of real (i.e. concrete) sounds from the everyday world. The technique is now absorbed into *electronic music.*

musizieren (G) To make music.

muso Colloquialism for a musician.

Mut, Muth (G) Courage, boldness.

muta (It) Change. A direction to change keys.

mute A device to change the tone and reduce the volume of an instrument.

muting Guitar technique in which the string is prevented

Muzak

m.v.

from ringing by damping with the picking or fretting hand.

Trademark name, now a generic term, for recorded background music in shops, etc.

'Mezza voce'. Half voice.

N

nach (G)   After.
Nachdruck (G)   Emphasis.
nachgehend (G)   Following.
nach hinten (G)   Upstage.
nachlassend (G)   Leaving behind. Slackening in speed.
Nachschlag (G)   'Afterstroke'. *Turn.*
Nachspiel (G)   'Afterplay'. *Postlude.*
Nachtanz (G)   'After dance'. In a *suite*, the quick dance used to follow a slower one.

Nachtmusik (G)   Night music.
Nachtstück (G)   Night piece. *Nocturne.*
nach und nach (G)   Gradually. Bit by bit.
nach vorn (G)   Downstage.
nach wie vor (G)   After as before.
nahe (G)   Near.
naïf, naïve (F), **naiv** (G)   Artless.
nakeres, nakers   Old English term for a small oriental *kettledrum*.
nämlich (G)   The same. Namely.
NARAS   National Academy of Recording Arts and Sciences. Body that presents Grammy Awards.
narrante (It)   Narrating. Declamatory.
Nashville   Nashville, Tennessee, the home of *Country and Western* music (*C&W*), and the showcase auditorium, the Grand Ole Opry.
naso, nasetto (It)   Nose.
Nationalhymne (G)   National anthem.
natural   A note that is neither raised (sharpened) nor lowered (flattened). The symbol that denotes this, thereby cancelling a *sharp* or *flat.*
naturale, nat. (It)   A direction to resume the normal method of performance.
natural minor   Minor scale consisting of a semitone interval between the second and third degrees, and the fifth and sixth. Also called pure minor or *Aeolian*. On C: C, D, E♭, F,G, A♭, B♭, C.
natürlich (G)   Natural.
N.C.   No chord.
Neapolitan sixth   In the key of C this chord (built on the flattened supertonic) contains the notes of the first inversion of a D♭ major triad. It is not the same as an *Italian sixth.*

neben (G)	Near, at the side of.
nebst (G)	Together with, including.
neck	The part of a string instrument to which the *fingerboard* is attached.
needle time	1960s (and later) term describing the proportion of broadcasting time that the unions permitted to be devoted to recorded music. Early records were played using needles.
negli (It)	In the, at the.
negligente, negligentemente (It)	Negligently.
nehmen (G)	To take.
nei, nel (It)	In the.
neighboring notes, neighbor notes	Occasionally called changing tones, this pair of embellishment notes first leaves a chord by a step in either direction, followed by a leap in the opposite direction, then resolves by a step to the original note.
nenia (It)	*Dirge.*
neo-classicism	Term applied to the anti-Romantic styles of Stravinsky, Hindemith and their contemporaries, during the 1920s and 1930s.
nera (It)	*Quarter note* or *crotchet*. Literally 'black'.
net, nette (F), **netto, netta** (It)	Clear.
neu (G)	New.
neumes	General term for the signs and symbols used for medieval musical notation.
New Age	Mid to late 80s style of music using electronic instruments and blandly fusing jazz and classical styles.
nicht (G)	Not.
nieder (G)	Down.
niederdrücken (G)	To press down, to depress.
Niederschlag (G)	Downbeat.
Niederstrich (G)	Downstroke (of bow).
niente (It)	Nothing.
ninna-nanna, ninnarella (It)	Cradle song.
ninth	The interval of nine *diatonic* steps. An octave and a second.
nobile, nobilmente (It)	Noble, nobly.
noch (G)	Still, yet.

noche (Sp)	Night.
noch einmal (G)	Once more.
noch zweimal (G)	Twice more.
noch langsammer (G)	Slower still.
nocturne (F),	Night piece.
notturno (It)	
node	A stationary point on a vibrating string or air column. On a string instrument, the point where *harmonics* are produced.
Noël, Nowell	Christmas, Christmas carol.
noire (F)	*Quarter note*, *crotchet*. Literally 'black'.
noise reduction system	An electronic device, used in recording and broadcasting, which will not pass low-level signals (noise, unwanted sound), only passing signals above a certain controllable threshold.
non (F), (It)	No, not.
None (G)	Ninth (interval).
nonet (Eng), **nonette** (F),	Ensemble of nine instruments.
nonetto (It)	
nonharmonic note	A note that is not part of the chord with which it sounds.
Nonnengeige (G)	*Tromba marina.*
non-transposing	An instrument that sounds as written. An instrument in C.
northern soul	Mainstream British popular music enjoying a vogue in northern clubs in the 1960s and 1980s.
nose flute	Small keyless wind instrument, blown by using the nostrils. The player's mouth (oral cavity) is used as a resonating chamber. Opening and closing the lips determines the pitch.
nota cambiata (It)	*Changing note.*
notation	Written music.
Note, Noten (G)	Note, notes. Written or printed music.
note head	The round part of the written note.
Notenbeispiel (G)	Musical example.
Noten lesen (G)	To read music.
Notenschrift (G)	Notation.
Notenständer (G)	Music stand.
note on/note off	The *MIDI* codes on synthesizers. Commands to the instruments they control.
notieren (G)	To notate.
notturnino (It)	Miniature *nocturne.*
nove (It)	Nine.

novelty song   A song with humorous words or music.

nun's fiddle   *Tromba marina.*

nuovo, nuova (It)   New.

nur (G)   Only.

nut   **1.** On string instruments, the ridge at the *pegbox* end of the *fingerboard*, over which the strings are stretched.
2. The held end of the *bow*, where the tensioning device is placed.

nutrendo, nutrito (It)   Sustaining, sustained. Literally 'nourishing', 'nourished'.

O

o	1. The symbol for an open string.
	2. Diminished.
	3. Triple time in medieval notation.
	4. Abbreviation for *ossia*.
OB	Outside Broadcast.
obbligato (It)	Obligatory. Traditionally indicates that an instrument has a compulsory, unusual and special role. Now frequently means the opposite to this - an optional solo or contrasting melody.
oben (G)	Over, above.
ober, obere (G)	Upper, higher, above.
Oberton (G)	*Harmonic, overtone.*
obligato	Incorrect spelling for *obbligato*.
oblique motion	Two melodic lines, one stationary, the other moving.
oblique stringing	Form of stringing used on upright pianos, to gain greater length of string.
oboe	*Double reed* conical bore *woodwind* instrument, in C.
oboe d'amore	An intermediate instrument, between the *oboe* and the *cor anglais*. Pitched in A.
ocarina (It)	Small keyless flute-like instrument, usually made from ceramic material, and shaped like an egg. Together with the protruding mouthpiece it has the appearance of a seated bird, hence the name, meaning 'little goose'.
octave	The distance between two frequencies that are related by the ratio 2:1. Interval between first and eighth notes of a diatonic major or minor scale, which have the same letter name.
octavin (F), **octavina** (It), **Oktavin** (G)	1. The *piccolo*.
	2. A small portable *spinet*.
	3. Small *guitar*, pitched an octave above normal.
	4. The fifteenth stop of the organ.
octet	1. A piece for eight instruments or voices.
	2. Eight performers.
octobass, octobasse	A double-size double bass, with stopping achieved by use of mechanical levers worked by hands and feet.
octuor (F)	*Octet.*

od (It)	Or.
ode	**1.** A chorus in a Greek play.
	2. A lyrical poem in the form of an address.
oder (G)	Or.
oeuvre (F)	Work. *Opus.*
offbeat	**1.** Normally unaccented beat. *Afterbeat, backbeat.*
	2. Unusual, unconventional.
off-Broadway	New York theater, away from Broadway, where the less popular shows are performed.
off-off-Broadway	The most radical and experimental New York theater.
offen (G)	Open.
offene Saite (G)	*Open string.*
offertoire (F)	*Offertorium.*
offertorium, offertory	**1.** A setting, in Latin, of biblical works, placed after the *Credo* in the Roman Catholic *Mass.* Performed while the Eucharist is being prepared and offered.
	2. Any music performed during offering.
öffnen (G)	To open.
ogni (It)	All, every.
ohne (G)	Without.
Oktave (G)	*Octave.*
Oktett (G)	*Octet.*
oliphant	A medieval horn traditionally made from the ivory of an elephant's tusk.
on cue	An instruction to begin playing at a specific signal or *cue.* The cue may be anything, but the instruction indicates that a cue or entry is determined or timed by what happens on stage. Usually encountered in theater or cabaret.
ondeggiando, **ondeggiante,** **ondeggiamente** (It)	Undulating. *Tremolo* or *vibrato.* Any swaying effect.
Ondes Martenot, **Ondes Musicales** (F)	Martenot Waves. The monophonic electronic instrument invented by Maurice Martenot (1898-1980).
ondulé (F)	Undulating. *Tremolo* or *vibrato.* Any swaying effect.
one-hit wonder	Pop star who achieves one big hit and is then forgotten.
one-step	A vigorous two-in-a-measure dance from immediately pre-World War 1, a feature of which was walking on tiptoe.

Ongarese (It)	Hungarian.
on sling	An instruction to *saxophone* players (sometimes to bass clarinetists) who double on *flute* or *clarinet* to have their saxophone (or bass clarinet) hooked on its sling in readiness for a quick change.
on the nose	Play without any preparatory upbeat or count-in. Mainly used in theater or cabaret.
op.	Abbreviation for *opus*.
open	**1.** Instruction to remove *mute*.
	2. Not stopped, fingered or fretted.
opener	An attention-getting piece to start a program. *Flag-waver*.
open form	Composition where the form is determined by the performer or conductor.
open harmonic	A *harmonic* played on an *open string*.
open harmony	When notes of a chord are not played in their closest positions, but every alternate note is shifted by an octave.
open notes	**1.** *Open strings*.
	2. On brass or woodwind instruments, notes produced without *crooks*, *keys*, *slides* or *valves*.
open strings	Strings that are not fingered, fretted or stopped.
Oper (G)	*Opera*, opera company.
opera	**1.** A dramatic work set to music, and where most of the text is sung with orchestral accompaniment, costumes and scenery.
	2. Plural of *opus*.
opera-ballet	Stage work giving equal importance to opera and ballet. Common in seventeenth and eighteenth century France.
opera buffa (It)	Comic opera.
opéra bouffe (F),	Comic opera, originally; later, French
opéra comique (F)	opera with spoken dialogue.
opera-oratorio	Stravinsky's term for his Oedipus Rex.
opera seria (It)	Serious opera.
operetta (It)	'Little opera'. Light opera.
opérette (F)	*Operetta*.
Opernhaus (G)	Opera house.
ophicleide (Eng),	Brass bass wind instrument with keys.
Ophikleide (G)	Now superseded by the *tuba*. A bass version of the *keyed bugle*.
opp.	Abbreviation for the plural of *opus*.

op. posth., or **op. post.**	Posthumous *opus*. A work published after the death of the composer.
opus (L)	Work. Followed by a number, is used to catalog a composer's output.
Opuszahl (G)	*Opus* number.
orageux, orageuse (F)	Stormy.
oration	Term occasionally used as a musical title.
oratorio	An extended setting of a religious text. Originally (early seventeeth century) for soloists, chorus and orchestra and performed with scenery. In later periods conceived and performed in a concert style.
Oratorium (G)	*Oratorio.*
Orchésographie (F)	A 1589 French treatise on dancing.
Orchester (G)	*Orchestra.*
Orchesterbesetzung (G)	*Orchestration*, orchestral forces.
Orchestergraben (G)	Orchestra pit.
orchestra	Large mixed body of instrumentalists.
orchestral score	*Full score.*
orchestration	The process of writing for an orchestra or band, or of adding instruments to a score written for another medium.
orchestre (F)	*Orchestra.*
orchestrion	Large barrel organ with pipes and percussion. A mechanical instrument intended to imitate the sound of the orchestra.
ordinaire (F)	Normal, ordinary. Used to rescind a direction to play in an unusual way.
ordinario (It)	Ordinary, normal.
Ordinary	Parts of the *Mass* that remain the same from day to day throughout the liturgical year.
ordre (F)	*Suite.*
organ	1. A keyboard instrument which sounds by sending air through pipes.
	2. An electronic instrument imitating the sound of the traditional wind-blown organ.
organetto	Fourteenth century portable organ.
organistrum	*Hurdy-gurdy.*
organum	Medieval polyphonic music.
Orgel (G)	*Organ.*
Orgelpunkt (G)	*Pedal point.*
orgia (It)	Orgy.
orgue (F)	*Organ.*

orgue plein (F)	Full organ.
orgue positif (F)	Choir organ.
ornament	A melodic embellishment, which may be inserted by the performer, or called for by the composer. These include *acciaccatura, appoggiatura, mordent, trill, turn.*
orpharion	Plucked wire-strung fretted instrument, of the *bandora* family.
orphéon (F)	French name for a male-voice choral society.
oscillator	An electronic device for generating cyclic waveforms. Used for sound generation in *synthesizers.*
osservanza (It)	Observation. Care.
ossia (It)	Or. Alternatively. (From 'o sia', 'or it may be').
ostinato (It)	Obstinate, persistent. Refers to an unyielding rhythmic or melodic figure.
ôter, ôtez (F)	Take off: ('ôtez les sourdines', take off the mutes).
ottava, ott. (It)	*Octave.*
ottava alta (It)	An octave higher.
ottava bassa (It)	An octave lower.
ottavino	1. *Piccolo.* 2. A small *virginal* or *spinet.*
ottone, ottoni (It)	Brass instruments.
oud, ud	Arab *lute.* A short-necked, unfretted, double strung lute played with a *plectrum.*
out, outside	A jazz expression referring to a style of playing or passage of music that is *atonal* or arhythmic.
out-chorus	Final *chorus* in a jazz performance, usually (but not necessarily) a recapitulation of the theme.
outro	Slang, derived as the opposite to *intro* (introduction).
ouvert, ouverte (F)	Open.
ouverture (F)	*Overture.*
overblow	On wind instruments, the technique of breaking the *fundamental* note to produce higher notes (*harmonics*).
overdrive	An electronic distortion effect produced by high signal levels.
overdub, overdubbing	To record a track on top of a previous track, in order to add more instruments or voices.
overstrung	A type of piano construction where the strings are set at two levels, crossing each other. This gives greater string length for a given size of instrument.

overtone

Any note of the *harmonic series* above the *fundamental*. Upper *partial*.

overtone series

The *harmonic series* above the *fundamental*.

overture

Introductory music.

P

_p_ (It) — Abbreviation for _piano_, soft.

p (F) — Pedal.

p (Sp) — Thumb, (_pulgar_).

pacato (It) — Calm, quiet.

pad —
1. Jazz and dance band slang term for a band library.
2. Soft sustained background chords in an arrangement.
3. _Drumpad._
4. Sixties slang for place of abode.

padiglione (It) — Tent, pavilion. The bell of a wind instrument.

paean — A song of praise.

pagode (P) — A gathering where _samba_ is played.

palcoscenico (It) — Stage.

palindrome — A word or phrase that reads the same backwards as forwards, e.g. 'Madam I'm Adam'. A similar reversal in music.

palotache — Hungarian instrumental piece in dance style, derived from the _verbunko_.

pan — A metal drum used in a _steel band_.

pandeiro (P) — Type of _tambourine_.

pandiatonic — A term coined by the twentieth century musicologist Nicolas Slonimsky, which he defines as '...free use of all seven degrees of the diatonic scale, melodically, harmonically or contrapuntally...' There is an absence of _chromatics,_ and use of the added sixth and ninth.

pandora — Type of _cittern._ Also _bandora._

pandurina — A small, wire-strung _lute._

panning — In _sound reinforcement_ (amplification), the movement of an audio signal between two speakers.

panpipes — Endblown pipes of graduated lengths (and hence graduated pitches), bound together in a row.

pantaleon, pantaleone, pantalon — An eighteenth century form of _dulcimer_ named after its inventor Pantaleon Hebenstreit. The name was borrowed to describe an early German _square piano. Pantaleon_ is also the name of a _clavichord_ stop.

pantomime — 1. Strictly, a musical play in which the story is portrayed only by gesture and movement. Dumb show.

2. British Christmas show, a stage performance loosely based on a fairy story or legend, interwoven with musical items and appearances by television entertainers and personalities.

paradiddle　A drum rudiment, a repeated sticking pattern where the strong beats are played with alternate hands.

parallel chords　The parallel movement of identical note combinations.

parallel fifths,　The movement of two voices, a fifth or an octave
parallel octaves　apart, in exact parallel in the same direction.

parallel intervals　The movement of two voices, at any interval, in exact parallel in the same direction.

parallel keys　Major and minor keys having the same *tonic*.

parameter　Originally a mathematical term, now (since the 1950s) used to describe basic compositional elements such as *pitch*, loudness, duration and *timbre*.

paraphrase　Term used to describe a type of jazz improvisation, where the original melody is played in a loose re-shaping.

Parkett (G)　Stalls.

parlando, parlante (It)　Speaking.

parlato (It)　Spoken.

part　**1.** The music for an individual voice or instrument.
2. A single melodic line in *counterpoint*.
3. A section of a work.

parte (It)　*Part.*

partials　*Harmonics* and *overtones* of the *harmonic series*.

Particell (G),　*Short score.*
particella (It)

Partie (G)　*Part*, rôle.

partie (F)　**1.** *Part.*
2. *Partita.*

partita (It), **partie** (F),　**1.** A set of *variations*.
Parthie (G)　**2.** A *suite.*

partition (F),　*Score.*
Partitur (G),
partitura (It)

partito (It)　Divided.

partsong　Unaccompanied *homophonic* composition for three or more voices.

part-writing   *Voice-leading* (German, *Stimmführung*). Skilful, melodic progress of each part.

pas (F)   **1.** Step. *Pas de deux*: stage dance for two performers.

2. No, not any.

paso doble (Sp)   Spanish dance in rapid 2/4 time. 'Double step.'

paspy   *Passepied.*

passacaglia (It),   A slow dance in triple meter, usually

passecaille (F)   having a repetitive bass line or theme.

passage-work   Slightly condescending term describing a portion of a composition that is regarded (by the observer) as filling or padding, frequently of a repetitive or virtuosic nature.

passaggio (It)   Passage. The alteration in muscle tension in the voice when changing register.

passend (G)   Fitting.

passepied (F)   French dance in fast triple time. *Paspy* in English.

passing note,   A note, approached and quitted by step,

passing tone   which connects two chord notes, but may itself be discordant with the prevailing harmony.

passio (L)   *Passion.*

Passion   The biblical story, as related in the Gospels, of the suffering and death of Jesus, set to music as an *oratorio*, and usually performed during the weeks before Easter.

Passione (It)   *Passion.*

pasticcio (It)   'A pie.' Operatic work comprised of music by different composers.

pastiche (F)   **1.** *Pasticcio.*

2. Piece in the style of another composer.

pastoral (Eng),   **1.** An instrumental movement in 6/8 or

pastorale (F), (It)   12/8 time, usually with a drone in the bass, intended to depict the music of shepherds.

2. A musical play on a rural subject.

patch   **1.** A set of *parameters* for a specific synthesized sound.

2. To connect pieces of electronic equipment together.

patchbay   Routing device for *patchcords*. In a studio, a number of sockets arranged in rows and columns.

patchcords   Short wires or cables used in a recording studio to make a connection in a *patchbay*.

patetico (It)   Pathetic.

pathétique (F)	Pathetic.
pathetisch (G)	Pathetic.
patimento (It)	Suffering.
patter song	Song with an abundance of words, uttered rapidly. A type of wordy solo comic song, heard in comedy or *operetta*, dependent on the rapid enunciation of syllables for its effect. The works of Gilbert and Sullivan provide many examples.
Pauke(n) (G)	*Kettledrum*, kettledrums.
pausa (It)	Rest. Not to be confused with *pause*.
pause	The sign instructing the player to hold a note or rest longer than normal. The sign is colloquially known as a bird's eye, or an eyebrow.
Pause (G)	**1.** A rest.
	2. An interval in a concert.
Pausenzeichen (G)	Rest sign.
pavan (Eng), **pavane** (F)	Sixteenth century slow dance in duple time.
paventato, paventoso (It)	Timid.
pavillon (F)	*Bell.* As in bell tent or pavilion, the *bell* of a clarinet, trumpet, horn, etc.
PCM	**P**ulse **C**ode **M**odulation. A technique of digital sampling.
peal	**1.** A set of tuned bells or chimes.
	2. The patterns of sounds emitted when a set of bells is rung.
peau (F)	Skin, of a drumhead.
pedal, ped.	**1.** A device controlled by the foot, such as on the organ, piano or harp.
	2. The *fundamental* or lowest note on a brass instrument.
	3. A note (usually the *tonic* or *dominant* of the prevailing key) sustained below changing harmonies.
pedal board	A keyboard played with the feet, for instance, on the organ.
Pedalcoppel (G)	Pedal coupler, on the organ.
pedale (It)	*Pedal* or pedals.
Pedalflügel (G)	*Pedal piano* (grand).
Pedalgebrauch (G)	Pedal use.
pédalier (F)	**1.** *Pedal board.*
	2. *Pedal piano.*
pedaliera (It)	*Pedal board.*
Pedalpauken (G)	Mechanically tuned *timpani*.

pedal piano	A piano fitted with a pedal keyboard. Written for by Schumann (1810-1856), and the French composers Alkan and Gounod.
pedal point	Alternative term for the harmonic device *pedal*.
pedal steel guitar	An electric guitar that is fixed horizontally onto a stand. Foot pedals are used to alter the tension of individual strings. Special *glissando* effects can be produced.
pedal tone	See *pedal point*.
peg, tuning peg	On a string instrument the dowel around which a string is wound, and which is rotated to tighten or slacken the string when tuning.
pegbox	The part of the head of a string instrument into which the tuning pegs fit.
peine (F)	Scarcely, hardly at all.
Peitsche (G)	Whip.
pénétrant (F)	Penetrating.
penillion (Welsh)	A type of traditional Welsh singing, wherein a well-known melody played on the harp accompanies verses sung in counterpoint.
penny whistle	*Tin whistle*.
pentachord	The first five notes of a diatonic scale.
pentatonic	Melody or harmony based on five notes. There are many pentatonic scales. Reference to 'the' pentatonic scale usually indicates a scale corresponding to the black notes on the piano, or a transposition thereof.
per (It)	By, through, for, in order to.
percussion family	Instruments that are shaken or struck to produce sounds of definite or indefinite pitch.
perdendo, perdendosi (It)	'Losing itself'. An instruction to play ever softer until inaudible.
perfect cadence	A *cadence* wherein the chord movement is V to I. *Full close*.
perfect interval	The standard intervals of a fourth, fifth and octave, e.g. C to F, C to G, and C to C.
perfect pitch	The ability to recognize a musical note without reference to an instrument.
performance practice	Translation from German, *Aufführungspraxis*. The understanding of conventions and historical knowledge needed to interpret a composer's intentions.

Performing Right Society (PRS)	The British agency which collects and distributes composer, arranger and publisher performance royalties.
period	A musical section or phrase often divided into two parts, *antecedent* and *consequent*.
però (It)	However, therefore.
perpetuum mobile (L)	Perpetually in motion.
pesant (F), **pesante** (It)	Weighing, heavy, heavily.
petit, petite (F)	Little.
petto (It)	Chest.
peu à peu (F)	Little by little.
pezzo (It)	Piece.
Pfeife (G)	Pipe.
pfiffig (G)	Artful.
Phantasie (G)	*Fancy,* reverie, *fantasy.*
phonofiddle	Violin in which the usual body is replaced by a metal amplifying horn. Said to have been used in the early days of gramophone recording.
phrase	A group of notes forming a unit of melody. Approximates to that which can comfortably be sung or played in one breath, or matches a sentence, or line of text.
Phrygian	A *mode* represented by the white keys on the piano, starting and finishing on E.
piacere (It)	Pleasure.
piacevole (It)	Agreeable, pleasant, easy.
pianamente (It)	Softly.
piangendo, piangente (It)	Weeping, plaintive.
piangevole, piangevolmente (It)	Plaintive, plaintively.
pianino	A small upright piano.
pianissimo, *pp* (It)	Very softly. The superlative of *piano.*
pianississimo, *ppp* (It)	Very, very softly.
piano, *p* (It)	Soft.
piano	*Pianoforte.*
piano à queue (F)	'Tailed piano'. Grand piano.
pianoforte (It)	Italian name for the piano. Literally 'soft-loud'. Keyboard instrument on which the keys operate felt hammers, which strike wire strings.
pianola	*Player piano.*
piano roll	Used by *player pianos.*
piano score	A (reduced) *score,* suitable for playing on the piano.

pianto (It)	Plaint, lamentation.
piatti (It)	*Cymbals.*
pibroch	A type of Scottish Highland bagpipe music. *Piobaireachd.*
picado (Sp)	A technique of *flamenco* guitar playing, where a fast scalic run is played with two fingers of the right hand.
Picardy third	*Tierce de Picardie.* A major chord ending a minor-key piece.
picchettato, picchiettato, picchiettando (It)	Knocked, knocking.
piccolo, piccola (It)	Little.
piccolo	A small flute an octave higher than the standard concert flute. It sounds an octave higher than written. A D♭ version exists.
pick	*Plectrum.*
Pickelflöte (G)	*Piccolo.*
pick scrape	The sound produced on a guitar by running a pick along the ridged covering of a wound string.
pickup	**1.** *Anacrusis.* The introductory notes preceding the strong notes of a new measure. **2.** A device that converts acoustic vibrations into electrical signals.
pieno, piena (It)	Full.
pietà, pietoso, pietosamente (It)	Pity, piteous, piteously.
piezo-electric transducer	A guitar *pickup* with a piezo-electric crystal.
pífano (P)	Primitive flute or *fife.*
pifferaro	A player of the *piffero.*
piffero	Italian instrument of the *shawm* family, alluded to by Handel in the music of the Pastoral Symphony in Messiah.
pikieren (G)	To play *spiccato.*
Pikkolo (G)	*Piccolo.*
pin bridge	A bridge, with holes through which strings are inserted and secured with pins on their ends. Usually guitar and bass guitar only.
pincé (F)	Pinched (*pizzicato*).
piobaireachd (Gaelic)	Scottish bagpipe music, tunes composed in memory of some historical event. Usually in the form of air with variations. See *pibroch.*
pipa	A Chinese *lute.*

pipe	**1.** To play a pipe.
	2. Hollow tube of any wind instrument.
	3. Instruments made from these tubes.
pipe organ	Keyboard and pedal board instrument using air under pressure to sound a series of pipes.
piqué (F)	'Pricked.' Same as *spiccato*.
piquiren (G)	To play *spiccato*.
piston	Valve on a brass instrument. In French the word is used as an abbreviation for *cornet à pistons*, the ordinary *cornet*.
pistone, pistoni (It)	*Piston*, pistons.
pitch	The musical equivalent of the technical term *frequency*.
pitch bend	A deviation in the pitch of a note.
pitch class	Term used in serial composition, for all notes of the same name.
pitch pipe	A small wind reed instrument used for providing a starting note for singers, or for instrumental tuning.
più (It)	More.
piuttosto (It)	Rather, somewhat.
piva (It)	*Bagpipe*.
pivot chord	In *modulation*, a chord that is common to both old and new keys.
pizzicato, pizz. (It)	'Pinched'. Plucking the string with the fingers.
PK. (G)	**1.** *Pauken*, *kettledrums* or *timpani*.
	2. *Pedalkoppel*, pedal coupler.
placido, placidezza (It)	Placid, placidity.
placito (It)	Pleasure.
plagal cadence	The *cadential* movement from chord IV to chord I. Its most familiar use is as the 'amen' of hymns.
Plagalschluß (G)	*Plagal cadence*.
plainchant, plainsong	Unaccompanied and unmeasured medieval *monophonic* chant. See *machicotage*.
plainte (F)	**1.** French ornament from seventeenth and eighteenth centuries. See *Nachschlag*.
	2. A slow piece which expresses sadness and lament.
plaisant (F)	Merry.
planchette ronflante (F)	*Thunder stick*.
plateau, plateaux (F)	Plate, plates. *Cymbals*.
platinum record	A recording that has sold a million copies. **Double platinum** means two million.

Platte (G)	Record.
plaudernd (G)	Chattering, babbling.
player piano	A piano with a mechanical or electro- mechanical device for playing prerecorded performances.
playlist	1. A list of records, determined by radio station managers to define what is played during a given week of broadcasting.
	2. Any list giving the order in which items are to be performed or recorded.
play the ink	A (verbal) direction to play the printed part and ignore any added longhand corrections or deletions.
plectrum	A pick for string instruments, usually of horn, plastic, ivory, metal or wood.
plein, pleine (F)	Full.
plein jeu (F)	Full organ.
pleno (It)	Full.
plop	On brass and wind instruments, a rapid slide downwards before a note.
plötzlich (G)	Suddenly.
pluck	To sound a string by pulling it with the fingers. See *pizzicato*.
plugging, to plug	Mid-twentieth century term for persistently performing a pop record on radio or television to increase its sales.
plunger, **plunger mute**	A rubber kitchen (plumber's) plunger which is held over the bell of a brass instrument (usually trumpet or trombone) to color the tone quality. Frequently used in combination with other mutes.
plus (F)	More.
pneuma (Greek)	Breath. In *plainsong*, a florid passage sung to a single vowel.
pochette (F)	Pocket. Small *violin*, (*kit*), tiny enough to be kept in the pocket. Formerly used by dancing masters.
pochettino, poch. (It)	Very slightly, very little.
pochissimo, poch. (It)	The least possible.
poco (It)	Little.
poco a poco (It)	Little by little.
poggiato (It)	Dwelt upon, leant upon.
pogo	A dance popular during the *punk rock* era of the 1970s. So named because the dancer imitated the effect of riding a pogo stick.

poi (It)	Then. After, afterwards.
point	**1.** The tip of the bow.
	2. Pedal.
pointé (F)	Pointed, detached.
pointillism	A painting term, referring to the use of dots (developed by the painter Georges Seurat (1859-91)). Applied to certain early twentieth century music where the notes are organized in 'dots' (isolated notes) rather than in a traditional melodic curve.
polacca (It)	*Polonaise.*
polka	An eighteenth century dance from Bohemia, in 2/4 time.
Polnisch (G)	Polish.
polo	A type of Spanish dance, with song, in triple time.
polonaise (F)	A Polish dance originating in the sixteenth century, in 3/4 time.
polychoral	A choir divided into two or more groups.
polychords	Chords combining separate triads.
polymetric	Simultaneous use of different meters.
polyphonic, polyphony	Several voices sounding simultaneously. 'Many voiced'. May apply equally to a Bach *fugue* or a *Dixieland* ensemble.
polyrhythm	Different rhythms played simultaneously.
polytonal, polytonality	Simultaneous use of different keys.
pommer	Type of *shawm.*
pompeux, pompeuse (F)	Pompous.
pompös (G)	Pompous.
pomposo (It)	Pompous, majestic.
ponderoso, pondoroso (It)	Ponderous.
ponticello (It)	The *bridge* of a stringed instrument. *Sul ponticello* means bowing at (on) the bridge.
pop	**1.** Abbreviation for popular, formerly used to describe (light orchestral) concerts that appealed to a wide general audience. Since the late 1950s pop has been used to describe commercial dance orientated music, with a heavy emphasis on vocalists. *Not* the same as *jazz,* or *rock.*
	2. Verb, to describe the clicking or snapping of one's fingers (in time to music).
	3. Distortion (popping) caused by a microphone being too close to a sound source.

pop cover	Sheath fitted over a microphone to prevent *popping*, or to eliminate wind noise.
port	The place on an electronic instrument or synthesizer where a cable is connected.
port-á-beul (Gaelic)	Mouth music, associated with Scotland.
portable keyboard	An electronic keyboard, that is light and easily carried.
portamento (It)	A slide or glide between notes.
portando (It)	Carrying.
portative organ	A small portable organ, from the Middle Ages.
portato (It)	Half staccato, between *staccato* and *legato*.
Posaune (G)	*Trombone.*
posément (F)	Steadily, sedately.
positif (F)	Choir organ, or chair organ.
position	1. On string instruments, the position of the left hand on the fingerboard.
	2. On the trombone, the position of the slide.
	3. The inversion of a chord.
	4. The spacing of a chord.
positive organ	A small medieval pipe organ, the pipes sounded by bellows which were pumped by a second person.
posizione (It)	*Position.*
possibile (It)	Possible.
post horn	A straight *bugle* sounded by mail coachmen to announce their arrival with the post.
postlude	1. An organ piece played at the end of a church service.
	2. The final item in a set of pieces.
potentiomer, pot.	A variable resistance. The term usually refers to the knob on a synthesizer or recording desk that controls this device.
pouce (F)	Thumb.
pour (F)	For.
poussé, poussez (F)	'Pushed.' Up-bow. Push on, go quicker.
pp	*Pianissimo.*
ppp	*Pianississimo.*
prächtig, prachtvoll (G)	Grand, grandly.
präcis (G)	Precise.
practise	British spelling of 'practice' used as a verb.
praeludium (L)	*Prelude.*
Prallender,	A short trill, related to the upper *mordent*.
Pralltriller (G)	
Präludium (G)	*Prelude.*

pratos (P)	*Cymbals.*
préambule	*Prelude.*
prebend (pre-bend)	A guitar technique where one bends a string before sounding it.
précédemment (F)	Previously.
precipitando,	Impetuously.
precipitato,	
precipitoso (It)	
précipité (F)	Impetuously.
preciso, precisione (It)	Precise, precision.
pregando (It)	Praying. In a devotional style.
preghiera (It)	Prayer.
prelude (Eng),	'Play before'. A piece played as an introduction.
prélude (F)	
préluder (F)	To prelude. Also, to tune up, or play a few introductory chords.
preludio (It)	*Prelude.*
premier, première (F)	First night, first performance.
prendre (F)	To take.
preparation	Preparing a *discord* by sounding the note in question as a *concord* before playing that same note as a *discord.*
prepared piano	A piano in which the tone has been changed by insertion of foreign objects on top of, or between, the strings. Usually associated with the work of John Cage, but first introduced by Henry Cowell (1897-1965), who was his teacher.
près (F)	Near.
presets	Standard combinations of certain settings that can be selected with a single control. Used on *organs* and *synthesizers.*
presque (F)	Almost.
pressando, pressante (It),	Pressing on. *Accelerando.*
pressant (F)	
pressez (F),	Increase speed.
pressieren (G)	
pressure,	In *synthesis*, a method by which certain effects (e.g.
pressure sensitivity	*vibrato*, *pitch bend*, *volume*) can be accessed. The pressure exerted upon the key controls that particular effect.
prestissimo (It)	Very fast.
presto (It)	Fast.
prick-song	To prick was to mark, or to write down. A song that

was written down or printed, rather than performed from memory or improvised. The idea of 'prick' in a musical sense still survives in the 'point' of 'counterpoint'.

prière (F) — Prayer.

prima (It) — First.

prima donna (It) — First lady. The most important female singer in an *opera*. Also used as a synonym for a difficult or self-important person.

primary chords, primary triads — Chords I, IV and V (*tonic*, *subdominant* and *dominant*) in any key.

prima vista (It) — First sight. *Sightreading*.

prima volta (It) — First time.

prime —
1. *Unison*.
2. The first note of a scale.

primo (It) —
1. First. The first part.
2. The upper part of a piano duet.

primo uomo (It) — First man. Chief male singer.

principal —
1. Instrumental section leader.
2. Singer who takes main parts in opera company.
3. *Diapason* type of organ stop.

print through — The effect of pre-echo or ghosting, caused by one layer of spooled tape recording (merely by being in contact) onto the next layer. As post-echo is less distracting than pre-echo, it is better to store spooled tape on the right hand, played, spool.

Probe (G) — Rehearsal.

proben, probieren (G) — To rehearse.

Probespiel (G) — *Audition*.

processional — Music performed for an entrance in procession.

program —
1. Instructions given to a computer.
2. To set those instructions.
3. A list of concert items, usually together with information about the works to be heard and those performing them.
4. A show on television or radio.

programme — British spelling of *program*.

program music, programmatic music — Illustrative music. Music that attempts to tell a story or paint a tone picture.

progression — Movement of one chord to another. *Chord sequence* is frequently and incorrectly used to describe a chord progression.

progressive jazz — A 1950s *modern jazz* style (e.g. Stan Kenton),

progressive tonality

associated originally with Californian musicians. Beginning a piece or movement in one key and ending in another.

progressivo, progressivamente (It)

Progressive, progressively.

prolation

Medieval musical term. A **major prolation** is the division of the whole note into three smaller time units. A **minor prolation** is the division of the whole note into two smaller time units.

prologue

Introduction presenting the background for an *opera* or dramatic work.

promo

Promotion.

promptement (F)

Promptly.

Proms

Abbreviation of Promenade Concerts, the annual London BBC summer concert series. The concerts began in 1895, and were conducted from then (until his death in 1944) by Sir Henry Wood. Though some of the audience stand, they do not promenade.

pronto (It)

Prompt, quick, ready.

Proper

Parts of the *Mass* whose texts change from day to day.

proposta (It)

The *subject* of a *fugue*.

prosody

The study of versification.

Prospekt (G)

Backcloth.

protest singer

Folk or folk-rock singer who specializes in politically orientated songs.

PS.

Short for *Posaunen*, trombones.

psalm

A sacred song or hymn, specifically one of the 150 in the Bible. Usually sung in *plainsong* form.

psalmody

The singing (or study) of *psalms*.

psalter

1. The Old Testament Book of Psalms.

2. Book of Psalms of the Reformed Churches in poetic verse settings, suitable for use by a congregation.

psaltery

An ancient, plucked, string instrument, similar to a *zither*.

public domain

Creative work (e.g. a composition, computer software) in which copyright has expired or has been relinquished by the owner.

Publikum (G)

Public, audience.

pulgar (Sp)

Thumb.

pull-off

A string instrument technique, sounding a note

135

	with the fretting finger after plucking the string, thus sounding the fretted (or open) note below it.
pulse	Sometimes taken to mean 'beat', but the two are not always synonymous.
Pult, Pulte (G)	Desk, meaning an orchestral music stand.
punk rock	A very simple but aggressive and hostile style of rock music and fashion, of the late 1970s. It accompanied the rise to fame of the Sex Pistols in 1976.
Punkt (G)	Dot.
punktiert (G)	Dotted.
punta (It)	The *point* of the *bow*.
punteado (Sp)	Plucked.
pupitre (F)	Desk. Music stand.
purfling	A decorative strip inlaid around the edges of the body of a string instrument.
pyiba	Chinese *lute*, pear-shaped, with four strings.
Pythagorean Comma	A tiny interval, about a quarter of a semitone, being the difference between B sharp and C natural, if a succession of perfect fifths is followed cyclically: C, G, D, A, etc.

Q

Q	*Regeneration* setting on a *filter*.
quadraphonic	A sound system, introduced in 1969, using four or more loudspeakers and four *signal* sources.
Quadrat (G)	*Natural* sign.
quadrille (F)	Early nineteenth century French square dance in five movements, which are alternately in six-eight and two-four time. The lancers is a type of quadrille.
quadruple meter	A *time signature* with four beats to a *measure*.
quadruplet	Four notes played in the time of three notes of equal value.
quail	A toy wind instrument, which imitates a quail.
Qual (G)	Agony.
qualvoll (G)	Agonized.
quantize	In *synthesis*, aligning notes to precise rhythmic values to smooth out inaccuracies.
quanto (It)	As much, so much.
quartal harmony	Harmony built up in fourths.
Quarte (G)	Fourth (interval).
quarter note	A note one quarter the duration of a whole note. *Crotchet*.
quarter tone	An interval of half a *semitone*.
quartet	1. A piece for four performers.
	2. Four performers.
Quartett (G)	*Quartet*.
quartetto (It)	*Quartet*.
quarto (It)	Fourth.
quasi (It)	Almost, as if, approximating to, like.
quatre, quatrième (F)	Four, fourth.
quattro (It)	Four.
quatuor (F)	*Quartet*.
quaver	Eighth note.
que (F)	That. As.
Queen (King), The	The British National Anthem.
quelque, quelques (F)	Some.
Querflöte (G)	Cross flute. The normal *transverse flute*.
questo, questa (It)	This.
queue (F)	Tail. Thus, *piano à queue* is a grand piano.
quickstep	1. A mid-twentieth century ballroom dance, to music played at around fifty measures per minute.
	2. A fast march.

quieto (It) — Quiet, calm.

quill — The part of the action of a harpsichord that plucks the strings.

quindicesima (*15ma*) — Fifteenth. Two octaves. Play two octaves higher than written.

quint — Organ stop sounding a note a fifth higher than the key depressed.

quinta (It), **Quinte** (G) — Fifth.

quintal harmony — Harmony built up in fifths.

quintet —
1. A piece for five performers.
2. Five performers.

Quintsaite (G) — E string of the violin.

quintuor (F) — *Quintet.*

quintupal meter — A *time signature* with five beats to a measure.

quintuplet — Five notes to be played in the time of four notes of equal value.

quitter (F) — To quit, to leave.

quodlibet (L) — 'That which pleases', or 'What is desired.' A group of pieces or songs, often humorous, assembled in ingenious or unusual fashion, and played simultaneously or successively.

quoique (F) — Although.

quote — A short phrase from a well-known tune inserted into a jazz improvisation.

R

R
1. Abbreviation for 'right', as in right hand.
2. Abbreviation for 'Royal', as in RNCM (Royal Northern College of Music).
3. Abbreviation for Ryom (Peter Ryom, b.1939) who compiled the catalog of the compositions of Vivaldi. R.V. = Ryom *Verzeichnis*.
4. Abbreviation (in French organ music) for *récit*, swell organ.

r
1. Abbreviation for *tonic sol-fa* symbol for the *supertonic,* i.e. the second degree of the scale.
2. 'Release bend' in guitar tablature.

rabab   *Rebab.*

rabbia (It)   Rage.

race recordings   Recordings made and marketed in North America to cater specifically for the taste of Afro-American audiences.

racket(t), rankett   A *Renaissance* double reed instrument, consisting of a short wooden cylinder containing an air channel pierced with holes. It has a limited scale and a deep sound. Later sometimes called the 'sausage bassoon', after the German *Wurstfagott*, and the French *cervelas* (saveloy).

raddolcendo, raddolcente (It)   Sweetening. Calming, becoming gentler.

raddoppiare (It)   To double.

radio microphone   A microphone with a built-in radio transmitter, thus needing no cable.

Radleier (G)   *Hurdy-gurdy.*

raffrenando (It)   Putting on the brake. Checking the speed.

raga, raag, rhag   In Indian classical music, a set of tones that establishes the melodic framework for a piece.

rageur (F)   Ill-tempered.

ragtime   A form of music popular in the 1890s. The name, and the genteel syncopation of the style, derives from 'ragged time'. The harmonies and form owe much to European marches and dance music. The piano music of Scott Joplin epitomizes the genre.

rake   1. A guitar technique involving dragging the *plectrum* (*pick*) across muted strings, and unmuting the last string so that it sounds.

	2. A sloping stage.
ralentir (F)	To slow down.
rallentare, rallentando,	Becoming gradually slower.
rallentato, rall. (It)	
RAM	Random-Access Memory.
Rampe (G)	Footlights.
R&B	*Rhythm and Blues.*
Rand (G)	Edge.
Rang (G)	Rank, order.
range	Compass. The span of the notes that an instrument or voice can produce.
rank	Set of organ pipes.
rap, rapping	**1.** Slang term for speech or conversation.
	2. Term used in *hip-hop* music to describe the singing or chanting of lyrics.
râpeur, rapeguero	*Güiro.* (Term used by Stravinsky.)
rapido, rapidamente,	Rapid, rapidly, rapidity.
rapidità (It)	
rappresentazione (It)	Representation, a staged action.
rapprocher (F)	To bring closer together.
rapsodia (It)	*Rhapsody.*
rapsodie (F)	Variant spelling of *rhapsodie.*
rasch, rascher (G)	Quick, quicker.
rasgado, rasgueado (Sp)	Strummed. A technique on the guitar, where the fingers strum the strings rapidly.
rasp	*Güiro.*
raspa (Sp)	A Cuban percussion instrument made from a gourd (seed pod), or a bamboo tube, with notches cut into it. A stick is scraped across these notches.
ratamacue	A drum rudiment, using an alternating hand sticking pattern.
Ratsche (G)	*Rattle.*
rattenere, rattenendo,	Holding back, slowing down.
rattenuto (It)	
rattle	**1.** Hollow container (originally a gourd or seed pod), fitted with a handle, and filled with lead shot, seeds, or other small hard objects. Sounded by shaking.
	2. A blade of hard wood or metal which is plucked by a notched wheel turned by a handle. Traditionally carried by football supporters, but used by orchestral percussion players.
rauh (G)	Rough, course.

rauschend (G)	Rustling, rushing, dashing.
rave	In the early 1960s, a party, also known as a **rave-up**. The term was revived in the 1980s, when the parties were on a grander scale, in disused barns, aircraft hangars, warehouses, etc. They were often organized secretly, and frequently involved drugs.
ravvivando, ravvivato (It)	Reviving, quickening, quickened.
ray, re	The second note of the major or minor scale.
real	Used as the opposite of *'tonal'*, i.e. an exact transposition of the subject, when discussing fugal *answers,* and *sequence.*
realize, realization	The performance (or notation) of a piece of music originally only notated in sketch form, such as in *figured bass*, or guitar chord symbols.
real-time mode	The actual time in which something takes place. Usually refers to human speed, as opposed to the speed at which a computer can function.
rebab	A small short-necked *violin* with two strings, from Northern Africa, Egypt and the Middle East.
rebec(k)	A medieval bowed string instrument, pear-shaped, with a short neck and three or four strings. Of Arab origin, it is a forerunner of the *violin*.
rebop	Early name for the type of modern jazz later known as *bebop*.
rebute (F)	*Jew's harp.*
recapitulation	**1.** The return to, or repetition of, a theme or passage. **2.** In *sonata form*, the final section, in which the themes reappear.
recessional	A piece played at the close of a church service, as the congregation departs.
rechts (G)	Stage right (opposite prompt).
recit.	Abbreviation of *recitative*.
récit (F)	Organ swell.
recital	Performance, usually by one or two performers only.
recitando, recitante (It), **récitant** (F)	Reciting.
recitative	Speech-like singing in *opera* or *oratorio*.
recorder	Wooden (nowadays frequently plastic) end-blown keyless flute.
reco-reco (P)	A notched instrument, usually of bamboo or metal, scraped with a stick.

recueilli (F)	Collected, meditative.
redend (G)	Speaking. Same as *parlando*.
redoubler,	To double, doubling.
redoublement (F)	
reduction	**1.** Piano reduction is an edition of an orchestral score produced for piano performance.
	2. Arrangement for reduced ensemble of a piece for large forces.
réduire (F),	To reduce, arrange.
reduzieren (G)	
redundant entry	In *fugue*, a voice that re-enters after all the entries of the *subject* and *answer*.
reed	A vibrating piece of cane, plastic or metal which produces a tone when activated by air. Reeds are *free* (e.g. in the *harmonica, accordion, harmonium*), or *fixed*, as in the *single reeds* used by *clarinets* or *saxophones*. *Double reeds* (fixed) are found in *oboes, bassoons* and *sarrusophones*.
reed-organ	Keyboard instrument using free-beating reeds and no pipes. See *harmonium*.
reeds	*Woodwind* section, particularly *saxophone* and *clarinet*.
reel	A lively Celtic dance.
reel-to-reel	An open-spool tape recorder, as opposed to a cassette recorder.
refrain	The chorus of a song, usually repeated.
refrapper (F)	To strike again.
regal	Sixteenth century portable *reed-organ*.
regelmäßig (G)	Regular.
regeneration	*Feedback.*
reggae	A Jamaican style of pop music from the mid-1960s, characterized by repetitive bass patterns and regular notes or chords played on an amplified rhythm guitar on the offbeat. Reggae often contains references to Rastafarianism.
Regie, Inszenierung (G)	Production.
Regisseur (G)	Director, producer.
Register (G),	**1.** Organ stop controlling a set of pipes.
register (Eng)	**2.** Range (register) of an instrument.
registration	The organization of a combination of stops and registers to produce a specific sound.
registro (It)	*Register.*
Reigen, Reihen (G)	Round dance, dance.

Reihe (G)	Row.
réjouissance (F)	Rejoicing.
relâché (F)	Loosened (e.g. of snare on *snare drum*).
related	A measure of one key's proximity to another. Keys that are close to each other are keys that are within one flat or sharp more or less. Thus D major (two sharps) is close to B minor (two sharps) and less close to B major (five sharps).
relative keys	Keys, major and minor, sharing the same *key signature*.
relative pitch	The ability to read or write music relative to the notes that have gone before, but without necessarily knowing the *absolute pitch* of those notes.
release	1. The end of a note. 2. The middle section of a standard song. Also called the *bridge* or *middle eight*.
religieux, religieuse (F)	Religious.
religioso, **religiosamente** (It)	Religious, sacred.
remaster	To issue a new recording using the original master disc.
remettre (F)	To put back.
Renaissance	Rebirth. Period from mid-fifteenth century to the end of the sixteenth century.
renforcer (F)	To reinforce.
rentrée (F)	Re-entry.
renvoi (F)	Sending back. The repeat sign.
repeat	Restatement.
repeat fee	An additional fee paid to broadcast performers when a recording is re-transmitted.
repente (P)	Improvised stanza sung by a *repentista*.
repentista (P)	*Troubadour*.
répétiteur (F), **repetitore** (It), **Repetitor** (G)	Musician who coaches and prompts the singers in an opera company.
répétition (F)	Rehearsal.
répétition générale (F)	Final dress rehearsal.
repiano	See *ripieno*.
repique (P)	Two-headed tenor drum in *samba*.
replica (It)	Repeat.
replicato (It)	Doubled.
repos (F)	Repose.

reprendre (F)	To take up again.
reprise (F)	Retaking-up.
	1. Replaying of an important theme or first section of a composition.
	2. In *binary form*, the return of the first section as the latter part of the second section.
Requiem Mass	Roman Catholic Mass for the Dead. The sections are: Introit, Kyrie, Gradual and Tract, Sequence (Dies Irae), Offertory, Sanctus, Agnus Dei, Communion and Responsory.
Requiemmesse (G)	*Requiem Mass.*
Requisit (G)	Prop.
residency	Having a regular engagement to perform at a venue.
residuals	Payments made for repeat performances.
résolument (F)	Resolutely.
resolution	The progression from *dissonant* to *consonant*. Resolving a *discord*.
resoluto, risoluto (It)	Resolute.
resoluzione (It)	*Resolution.*
resonance	**1.** The transmission of vibrations from one object to another.
	2. In *synthesis*, the *regeneration* setting on a *filter*.
Resonanztisch (G)	*Soundboard.*
resonator	Anything that reinforces sound by *resonance*.
resonator guitar	*Dobro.*
response	**1.** In a *fugue*, the *answer*.
	2. An answer to a call. Call and response is also known as *antiphony*.
ressortir (F)	To come out. To make a melody prominent.
rest	**1.** A period of silence.
	2. Symbols that indicate silence.
restez (F)	Remain. Remain in one (hand) position, or to remain on one note.
resultant tone	Resultant tones are of two types, difference tones and summation tones. When two notes are sounded, a third note may sometimes be heard. This note is either the difference between the two sounded tones (when it will be lower in pitch than either of them), or the sum of the two tones, when it will be higher than the two sounded.
retardation	**1.** Gradually slowing, holding back.
	2. In jazz, the placing of harmonic change slightly

late in terms of the *harmonic rhythm* of the piece, having the twin effects of holding back and increasing *dissonance*.

retenant, retenu (F)   Holding back, held back.

retrograde   Playing a melodic line (or any other musical idea) backwards.

reveille   Awakening. A military wake-up call, played by a bugler.

reverb, reverberation   1. The rebounding of sound, *echo*.
2. An electronic effect that imitates the above.

reverberation time   Defined as 'the time a sound event will take to decrease in amplitude by 60 decibels.'

rf., rfz.   *Rinforzando*. A reinforced accent.

R.H.   Right Hand. Indication for keyboard players.

rhapsodie (F),   A free style instrumental piece.
Rhapsodie (G), **rhapsody**

Rhodes piano   An electric piano, named after its inventor, Harold Rhodes. Also called *Fender-Rhodes*.

rhumba   *Rumba*.

rhythm   Everything concerning the time aspect of music.

rhythm and blues   Form of pop music that originated in the 1940s, and was the precursor of *rock 'n' roll. R & B*.

rhythm changes   The *chord progression* (not *sequence*) of the George Gershwin tune 'I Got Rhythm'. This harmonic foundation was used for many subsequent modern jazz 'originals', such as *Oleo*, *Anthropology*, etc.

rhythm machine   *Drum machine*.

rhythm section   Bass and drums, usually with piano and /or guitar, forming the self-contained section that provides rhythm and harmony for a soloist in jazz and popular music.

ribs   The sides of a string instrument, joining the back and front.

ributhe (Scottish)   *Jew's harp*.

ricercar, ricercare (It)   To seek again. Instrumental music of the sixteenth and seventeenth centuries, in *contrapuntal* style.

richettato (It)   Same as *spiccato*.

richtig (G)   Right. Precise.

ride cymbal   The main *cymbal* of a jazz drum set.

ridotto (It)   Reduced. Arranged.

riduzione (It)   *Reduction*.

riff   A repeated melodic pattern, much used in the jazz of the 30s and 40s, particularly in the bands of Fletcher Henderson and Count Basie. Sometimes (wrongly) used as a synonym for *lick*.

rigadoon (Eng),
rigaudon (F) — A seventeenth and eighteenth century French dance in 2/2 time that became part of the *suite*.

rigore, rigoroso (It) — Rigor, rigorous.

rilasciando,
rilasciante (It) — Releasing, relinquishing, i.e. getting gradually slower.

rimettendo,
rimettendosi (It) — Putting back. Resuming the old tempo.

rim shot — A loud percussive stick stroke on the rim of a *snare drum*.

rinforzando, rinforzato,
rinf., rfz., rf. (It) — Reinforcing. A reinforced accent.

rip — A loud *glissando* into the beginning of a note.

ripetizione (It) — Repetition.

ripieno (It) — Replenished. The full orchestra as opposed to the solo group or *concertino*. Ripieno is frequently misspelled and mispronounced as *repiano*.

riposo, riposato (It) — Relaxed, quiet.

riposta (It) — The *answer* in a *fugue*.

riprendere (It) — To take up again.

ripresa (It) — Repeat.

risoluto (It) — Resolute.

ristringendo (It) — Drawing-together. Quickening.

risvegliato (It) — Wakened up.

ritardare, ritardando,
ritard., rit. (It) — Delaying. Becoming gradually slower.

ritenuto, riten., rit. (It) — Held back. Immediately slower.

ritmico (It) — Rhythmic.

ritmo (It) — Rhythm.

ritornello (It) — Little return.
1. A *refrain*.
2. The return to the full orchestra (*tutti*) in a *Baroque* concerto.

ritornello form — A piece or movement based on recurring passages.

roadie — Road manager, a member of the team which maintains, transports and sets the equipment for a touring band or ensemble.

rock, rock 'n' roll — A type of popular music that first appeared during the 1950s, originally in America, with the emphasis on voice and guitar, both amplified.

rock tupiniquim (P) — Pejorative nickname for Brazilian rock music.

roco (It)	Raucous.
rococo	A decorative and ornamental style of eighteenth century art, succeeding the *Baroque*.
roh (G)	Rough. Course.
Rohr (G)	*Reed.*
roll	A continuous sound on a drum, produced by a rapid succession of strokes.
Rolle, Partie (G)	Rôle.
rolled, rolled chord	Instruction or description of a piano technique adopted to cope with intervals that are too large for the performer's handspan, e.g. the interval of a tenth in the left hand may be too great for a pianist to span cleanly, but can be played if the notes are sounded consecutively rather than simultaneously.
Rolltrommel (G)	Tenor drum.
ROM	Read Only Memory.
romance (Eng), romanza (It), Romanze (G)	Imprecise term, implying music of a gentle or tender nature.
Romantic, Romanticism, Romantik (G)	Movement, current in the arts from the late eighteenth century and through most of the nineteenth century, which emphasizes feelings and emotions.
rombando (It)	Humming.
ronda, rondalla (Sp)	Outdoor music, performed by young men who tour the streets and play in front of people's houses.
ronde (F)	Whole note.
rondeau (F)	1. *Rondo.* 2. Form of medieval French poetry set to music. Usually includes a *refrain* and a *verse*.
rondel (F)	*Rondeau.*
rondo (It)	A form in which a theme recurs in alternation with contrasting themes, usually in the pattern ABACADA or ABACABA.
root	The fundamental note of a chord, though not necessarily at the bottom (the bass) of that chord.
root position	When the *root* of a chord is the lowest note, the bass.
roqueiro (P)	Rocker.
rosalia (It)	Alternative name for a *real sequence*. A real sequence occurs at the beginning of traditional Italian song 'Rosalia mia cara'.
rose, rosette	Decoration around the *soundhole* (of a guitar, etc.).

147

rosin	A tablet of hardened tree-resin, rubbed onto the bows of string instruments to increase the friction between bow and string. See *colofonia, Kolophon.*
rota	1. A *round.*
	2. Latin name for the *hurdy-gurdy.*
rote, rotta	A type of plucked lyre, from the Middle Ages. Another name for *crwth.*
rotondo (It)	Round. Full in tone.
Rototom	Commercial name for a tunable drum in which the tuning is achieved by rotating the head.
roulade (F)	An ornamental vocal phrase.
round	A continuous *canon*, for two or more voices, usually sung in *unison* or *octaves.*
round and round	Usually in theater music or cabaret, a short section repeated *ad nauseam*, and beyond.
roundelay	*Rondeau.*
rovescio, al (It)	In reverse.
row	Abbreviation of *tone row.*
rub	Close interval inside block harmony, as in 'minor second rub'.
rubato, tempo rubato (It)	Robbed. To play time values freely, with give and take.
rubible	*Rabab, rebec.*
Rücksicht (G)	Consideration.
rudement (F)	Roughly.
rudiments	The basic sticking patterns used by percussionists. See *drag, flam, paradiddle, ratamacue, roll* and *ruff.*
rueda (Sp)	Spanish round dance, in five-in-a-measure time.
ruff	Drum rudiment. A note preceded by two *grace notes.*
ruhelos (G)	Restless.
Ruhepunkt, Ruhezeichen (G)	Rest point, rest sign.
ruhig, ruhevoll (G)	Peaceful, calm.
Rührtrommel (G)	Tenor drum.
Rührung (G)	Feeling.
rumba	Afro-Cuban dance, the music for which has a characteristic 8/8 time pattern of 3+3+2. It has been observed that the dance is not suggestive, as it leaves nothing to suggest!
Rundfunk (G)	Broadcast, radio.
Russian bassoon	*Serpent.*

russo, russa (It)   Russian.

rustico (It)   Rustic, rural.

Rute, Ruthe (G)   Rod. Switch. Instruction (in German-language scores) to drummer to change to wire brushes.

ruvido (It)   Rugged, harsh.

rythme, rythmique (F)   Rhythm, rhythmic.

S

S	Abbreviation for: *segno, senza, sinistra, sol, solo, soprano, sordini, subito.*
s	*Tonic sol-fa* symbol for *soh*, the fifth degree of the scale.
SAB	Abbreviation for Soprano, Alto, Baritone.
saccadé (F)	Jerked. Sharply accented.
sackbut, (sacbut, sagbut)	Forerunner of the *trombone*.
saddle	A part of the *bridge* of the guitar.
saeta (Sp)	Unaccompanied Spanish folk song from Seville, sung at Easter.
Säge (G)	Saw.
Saite (G)	String.
Darmsaite (G)	Gut string.
leere Saite (G)	*Open string.*
Metallsaite (G)	Metal string.
Saitenhalter (G)	Tailpiece on violin.
salmo (It)	*Psalm.*
Salonstück (G)	Drawing room piece.
salsa	Latin American music that combines Latin rhythms with rock.
saltando, saltato (It)	Jumping, leaping. A string bowing technique where the bow is bounced on the string.
saltarello	Italian dance incorporating jumps.
samba	Music and dance from Brazil.
sambista (P)	Someone who sings, writes, plays or dances *samba* almost exclusively.
samisen, shamisen	Japanese flat-backed long-necked *lute*, with three strings. The term is incorrectly used to describe a percussion instrument in Puccini's Madam Butterfly. Also found in southern China. Mostly used in entertainment.
Sammlung (G)	Collection.
sample	1. In *synthesis*, a digital recording of a sound. 2. A small portion of an existing recording that is *mixed* into a new recording.
sampler	Device for the digital recording of analog sound.
sämtlich (G)	Complete, collected.
Sanctus (L)	Holy. Part of the *Mass*.
sanfona (P)	*Accordion*, button accordion.
sanft (G)	Soft.

Sänger (G)	Singer.
sans (F)	Without.
sansa	*Mbira.*
saraband (Eng),	Slow dance in triple time. Part of the *Suite.*
sarabande (F)	
sarangi	A northern Indian *violin*, with a short neck, three or four bowed strings, and sympathetic strings.
sardana (Sp)	Catalonian national dance. See *cobla.*
sarod	An Indian plucked-string instrument, without frets. Has *drone* strings and *sympathetic* strings.
sarrusophone	A double reed instrument with a brass body and conical bore. Made in various sizes. Bassoon fingering is used.
sassofono (It)	*Saxophone.*
SATB	Abbreviation of Soprano, Alto, Tenor, Bass.
Satz (G)	**1.** A musical setting. Thus *Tonsatz*, note setting.
	2. Movement, number.
	3. A theme or subject. Thus *Hauptsatz*, main theme; *Nebensatz*, subsidiary theme.
saudade (P)	Wistful remembrance. Longing.
sausage bassoon	*Racket. Cervelas.*
sautillé (F)	Springing. *Staccato* bowing technique in which the bow bounces off the string. *Saltato.*
saw	*Musical saw.*
sawtooth wave	In *synthesis*, a *waveform* where the voltage changes slowly in one direction, and abruptly in the other. The sound produced is bright and buzzy.
sax	*Saxophone.* An abbreviation less used by saxophonists than by others.
saxhorn	Keyed brass *bugle*, produced in various sizes and pitches. Invented by Adolphe Sax (1814-1894).
saxofonia, saxofono (It),	*Saxophone.*
Saxofon (G)	
saxophone	Keyed brass single reed instrument with a conical bore and a range of two and a half octaves or more, depending on the performer. Member of the woodwind family, invented by Adolphe Sax around 1840. Made in various sizes, from the rare *contrabass* to the tiny *sopranino*. The *alto* in E♭ and the *tenor* in B♭ are the most popular.
sbalzato (It)	Jerk, dash.
scacciapensieri (It)	*Jew's harp.*
scale	The word derives from the Italian word for

151

	stairway or ladder, 'scala', and is a progression of single notes (up or down) in steps.
scale degree	The names and numbers of each note in the *scale*.
scalic	Adjective used to describe an approach to jazz improvisation, as opposed to arpeggiated.
scaling	In *synthesis*, the degree to which a *parameter* influences a function.
scat, scat singing	Vocal jazz improvisation, using nonsense words.
scemando (It)	Diminishing.
scena (It)	Stage, scene.
Schale, Schalen (G)	*Cymbal, cymbals.*
schalkhaft (G)	Roguish.
Schall (G)	Sound, peal, ring.
Schallbecken (G)	*Cymbals.*
schalldicht (G)	Soundproof.
schallen (G)	To sound, peal, ring.
Schallplatte (G)	Record.
Schalltrichter (G)	Bell (of a wind instrument).
Schalltrichter in die Höhe (G)	Bells up. Lift the bell high. Instruction to wind players.
Schalmei (G)	*Shawm.*
scharf (G)	Sharply, harsh, rigorous.
Schärfe (G)	Sharpness.
schaurig, schauerlich (G)	Ghastly, gruesome.
Schauspiel (G)	Play (theatrical).
Schauspieldirektor (G)	Impresario.
Scheinwerfer (G)	Spotlight.
Schelle (G)	Bell. A small bell, such as a *sleigh bell.*
Schellenbaum (G)	*Bell tree. Turkish crescent.* See *jingling Johnny.*
Schellengeläute (G)	Bell-ringing.
Schellentrommel (G)	Bell-drum. A *tambourine.*
schelmisch (G)	Roguish.
scherzando (It)	Playful, light-hearted.
scherzare (It)	To joke.
scherzo, scherzi (It)	Joke, jokes.
	1. A piece in lively tempo.
	2. A movement (of a *symphony, sonata,* etc.) in fast triple time. It replaced the *minuet.*
scherzoso (It)	Same as *scherzando.*
schietto (It)	Sincere, unadorned.
Schifferklavier (G)	*Accordion.*
Schlacht (G)	Battle.

Schlag (G) — Stroke, blow.

Viertelschlag (G) — Quarter note beat.

Schlägel (G) — Drumstick.

schlagen (G) — To strike.

Schlager (G) — Pop song (i.e. a hit).

Schlaginstrument (G) — Percussion instrument.

Schlagzeug (G) — Kit percussion (jazz, rock).

Schlagzither (G) — Striking-zither, a form of *dulcimer* (not a *zither*) in which the strings are struck instead of plucked. *Hackbrett*.

Schlangenhorn (G) — *Serpent.*

Schlangenrohr (G) — *Serpent.*

Schlegel (G) — *Schlägel.*

Schleifer (G) — *Slide.*

schleppen (G) — To drag.

schleppend (G) — Dragging.

Schlummerlied (G) — Slumber song. *Lullaby.*

Schluss (G) — Conclusion. End.

Schlüssel (G) — Clef. (A literal translation is 'key', but this is not the musical meaning.)

Schlusssatz (G) — Final section.

Schlusszeichen (G) — Close-sign. *Double bar* with pause at the end of a repeated section, denoting the end of a movement.

schmachtend (G) — Languishing.

schmaltz (Yiddish) — Fat, melted grease (from German, *Schmalz* - 'fat'). Vulgar sentimentality.

schmeichelnd (G) — Coaxingly.

schmelzend (G) — Melting. Dying away.

Schmerz (G) — Pain, sorrow.

schmetternd (G) — Blared. Instruction to horn players to produce *stopped* notes (hand in bell) with hard blowing. Also indicated by + together with ff.

Schnarre (G) — *Rattle.*

Schnarrsaite (G) — *Snare.*

Schnecke (G) — Snail. *Scroll*, of a string instrument.

schneidend (G) — Cutting sharply. Defining.

schnell (G) — Fast.

schneller (G) — Faster.

Schneller (G) — A variety of *mordent.*

Schola Cantorum (L) —
1. A school of Roman monks who helped popularize *Gregorian chant.*
2. Name used by many choirs.
3. Famous *conservatoire* in Paris founded by Vincent d'Indy in 1894.

schön (G)	Beautiful.
Schottische (G)	Scottish. (Pronounced in English without sounding the final 'e'). A round dance similar to the *polka*.
Schräge (G)	*Rake*, of a sloping stage.
Schrammel quartet	Austrian (Viennese) light-music ensemble, comprising two violins, (or violin and clarinet) guitar (or *zither*) and accordion. Other variants are Schrammel Orchestra and Schrammkapelle. The name comes from the founder, Johann Schrammel (1850-1893).
schrittmässig,	Step-style, step-wise. At a walking pace.
schrittweise (G)	The same as *andante*.
schütteln (G)	To shake.
schwach (G)	Weak.
schwächer (G)	Weaker.
schwankend (G)	Swaying.
Schwebung (G)	Fluctuation.
	1. *Beats* between two slightly mistuned notes.
	2. Tremulant stop on the organ.
Schweigen (G)	Silence. To be silent.
schwellen (G)	To swell.
schwer (G)	**1.** Heavy in style.
	2. Difficult.
schwerer (G)	Heavier.
schwerfällig (G)	Heavy, deliberate.
schwermütig,	Heavy-hearted.
schwermutsvoll (G)	
schwindend (G)	Diminishing.
Schwung (G)	*Swing*.
schwungvoll (G)	Sweeping, lively, with zest, vigor or verve, with a flourish.
scintillante (It)	Sparkling.
sciolto, scioltamente (It)	Easy, free.
scivolando (It)	Sliding.
scoop	A very short *glissando* upwards into a note, usually in a jazz context. See also *bend, smear, glide*.
scordato (It)	Out of tune.
scordatura (It)	Mis-tuning. Changing the tuning of a string from the normal.
score	Written music that shows the whole of the music, as distinct from a *part* for one performer. See also *full score, miniature score, orchestral score, piano score, vocal score*.

scorewriter

Computer software for writing, printing and playing music. Well-known commercial types include Sibelius, Encore, Cubase and Finale.

scoring

1. Composing the music for a film or show.

2. A synonym for *orchestration*.

scorrendo, scorrevole (It)

Scouring. Gliding or flowing, scurrying.

Scotch snap (Scots snap)

A sixteenth note followed by a dotted eighth note.

scozzese (It)

Scottish.

scratching

The art of manipulating a record (originally *vinyl*, now *CD*) with a back and forth movement of the record turntable to create a rhythmic scratching sound.

screech trumpet

Very high trumpet playing, usually in a *big band* or jazz orchestra context. Cat Anderson and Maynard Ferguson were notable exponents.

screw

In the bow of a stringed instrument, the mechanism that tightens the bow hair.

scroll

The carved head of a string instrument. In Germany its curly shape has earned it the name *Schnecke,* a snail.

scucito (It)

Unsewed. Disconnected.

sdegno (It)

Disdain.

sdrucciolando (It)

Sliding.

sec, sèche (F)

Dry. To strike and release a chord immediately.

secco (It)

Dry. Unornamented. *Recitativo · secco* (dry recitative) is recitative accompanied only by *harpsichord* and other *continuo* instruments.

sechs (G)

Six.

Sechzehntel, Sechzehntelnote (G)

Sixteenth, sixteenth note. *Semiquaver.*

second

1. The interval between two consecutive degrees of the diatonic scale.

2. The name given to the instrument performing a lower-pitched part, as in *second violin* or *second clarinet.*

secondando (It)

Seconding. Same as *colla voce.*

secondary dominant

A *dominant seventh* chord built on any note other than the fifth degree of the home key.

Second Chicago School

Free jazz movement of the late 1960s, based in Chicago, including Anthony Braxton, Muhal Richard Abrams and Sun Ra.

second inversion

A chord with the fifth as its lowest note. Six-four chord.

secondo, seconda (It)	Second. The lower part in a piano duet.
Second Viennese School	Schoenberg, Berg and Webern and their followers. See *serial music*.
secular music	Non-religious music. As opposed to sacred music.
Seele (G)	Soul. *Soundpost* (of a string instrument).
segno (It)	Sign.
segue (It)	Follows. Go on without a break, continue immediately.
seguendo, seguente (It)	Following.
seguidilla(s) (Sp)	Type of ancient Spanish dance, in quick three-in a-measure time.
Sehnsucht (G)	Longing.
sehr (G)	Very.
sei (It)	Six.
Seises (Sp)	Choirboys who sing, dance and play *castanets* in the cathedral of Seville on certain festival days. Comes from 'seis', six, but numbers now vary.
Seite (G)	Side.
Seitenbühne (G)	Wings (theatrical).
semibiscroma (It)	Sixty-fourth note.
semibreve	Whole note.
semi-chorus	A section of a choir.
semicroma (It)	Sixteenth note.
semiquaver	Sixteenth note.
semitone	Half step in pitch.
semplice (It)	Simple.
sempre (It)	Always.
sensibile, sensibilità (It)	Sensitive, sensitivity.
sentito (It)	Felt.
senza (It)	Without.
senza vib. (It)	Without *vibrato*.
séparé (F)	Separated.
sept (F)	Seven.
septet	1. A piece for seven performers. 2. Seven performers.
septième (F)	Seventh.
septolet	*Septuplet*.
septuplet	Seven notes played in the time of four, or six.
sequence	The repetition of a phrase at a higher or lower pitch. A *real sequence* is an exact repetition. A *tonal sequence* is a repetition altered to remain within the key. See *rosalia*.
sequencer	In *synthesis*, a device that records and plays back incoming *MIDI* information in the order it occurs.

sequential	In the manner of a *sequence*.
serenade	A love song or piece traditionally performed in the evening, in the open air, below the loved one's window.
serenata	1. Italian for *serenade*.
	2. A type of *cantata*.
	3. An instrumental *suite*.
serenatella (It)	Diminutive of *serenata*.
sereno, serenità (It)	Serene, serenity.
serial music	A method of composition based on *twelve-tone technique* (*dodecaphony*), encompassing not only pitch but note durations, dynamics, etc., strictly ordered. Associated with Arnold Schoenberg and other members of the *Second Viennese School*.
seriamente (It)	Seriously.
series	The set of notes on which a twelve-tone composition is based. The order is all-important. However, it can be inverted or reversed.
sérieux, sérieuse (F)	Serious.
serio, seria, serioso, seriosa (It)	Serious.
seriosamente (It)	Seriously.
serpent	An ancient and obsolete member of the horn family, having an S-shaped wooden body with finger holes and keys, and a cup mouthpiece.
serpentone (It)	*Serpent.*
serrando, serrato (It)	Pressing, pressed. Getting quicker. Tightened.
serrant, serré (F)	Increasing speed and tension. *Stringendo*.
SESAC	Society for European Stage Authors and Composers. A royalty collecting organization.
sestetto (It)	*Sextet.*
sette (It)	Seven.
seufzend (G)	Sighing.
seven-string guitar	A *guitar* with an additional string. This may be a higher string, usually tuned to A, or an additional lower string, usually tuned to D.
seventh	Interval taking seven steps in the major or minor scale, counting the bottom and top notes.
seventh chord	Chord containing root, third, fifth and seventh degrees. The description is imprecise as to the type of chord.
severo, severamente (It)	Severe, severely.
Sevillana(s) (Sp)	Lively Andalusian *flamenco* song and dance.

sextet	1. A piece for six performers.
	2. Six performers.
sextolet	*Sextuplet.*
sextuor (F)	*Sextet.*
sextuplet	Six notes played in the time of four of equal value.
sfogato (It)	Evaporated. To play in an airy, delicate way.
sfoggiando (It)	Flauntingly, ostentatiously.
sforzando, sforzato,	Forcing, forced.
sfz., sf. (It)	
sforzando-piano, sfp. (It)	Accent, then immediately soft.
shahnai	North Indian reed instrument. A version of the *shawm*.
shake	Type of *trill*.
shaker	Hollow hand-held percussion instrument, filled with seeds or lead shot, shaken to produce a sound.
shakuhachi	Japanese end-blown flute, traditionally made from bamboo, now available in plastic.
shank	Part of a wind instrument, between the mouthpiece and main body. See *crook*.
shanty	Sailor's work song. The word is probably derived from the French, *chanter*, to sing.
sharp	1. The symbol ♯, instructing the performer to raise the pitch of a note by one half step.
	2. High in pitch.
shawm	Double reed woodwind instrument, forerunner of the *oboe*.
sheet music	Printed music, usually the piano copy of a *standard* or a pop tune.
shell seventh	Jazz term for two-note left hand piano voicing containing only the root and flattened seventh of the chord.
sheng	A Chinese *mouth organ*, with a wind chamber, pipes, and free reeds.
shift, shifting	Changing the position of the fingering hand on string instruments.
shimmy	Early twentieth century American dance, referred to in the song 'I Wish That I Could Shimmy Like My Sister Kate', recorded by Louis Armstrong and others.
sho	A Japanese *mouth organ* similar to the *sheng*.
shofar, (shophar)	An ancient Hebrew wind instrument, made from a ram's horn, used in the synagogue.
short octave,	The omission of certain low notes (C

(broken octave)	sharp, D sharp, F sharp, G sharp) on the keyboard of the organ. In the days before *equal temperament* these notes were impossible as key notes, and were therefore omitted from the instrument to save money. The device applied to other keyboard instruments.
short score	*Reduction. Score* produced for piano performance.
shout, shout chorus	**1.** In big band or jazz orchestra writing, it is an exuberant climactic brass-led passage. **2.** A lively type of piano playing in the *stride* style, as in James P. Johnson's 'Carolina Shout' of 1921. **3.** A *blues* shouter is a rough performer who shouts the blues rather than sings them.
shuffle	**1.** A nineteenth century dance step from the Southern United States. **2.** An early jazz rhythm, in a skipping style, approximating to a literal expression of the uneven triplets of 12/8 time, rather than the smoothed-out and less easily quantified 'swung-eighth' subdivisions that came later. Shuffle has been employed in subsequent jazz styles.
si	**1.** The fifth degree of the diatonic scale (*soh*) raised a half step. **2.** Another name for the seventh degree of the diatonic scale, an alternative to *ti*.
sibilance	Prominence of fricative consonants ('ess' sounds), such as 'ch' and 's', a particular problem in sound reproduction and *sound reinforcement*.
sich schminken (G)	To make up.
sich verbeugen (G)	To (make a) bow. (Acknowledgement.)
siciliano, siciliana (It), **sicilienne** (F)	A song or instrumental piece, commonly in 6/8 or 12/8 time, supposedly of Sicilian origin.
side	One face of a disc. Term used in the 78 rpm era.
side drum	*Snare drum.*
sideman	Musician in a jazz ensemble who is neither the leader nor a featured soloist.
sideslip	A device in jazz improvisation, where the soloist immediately repeats a short *lick*, but transposed up or down a semitone. Creates harmonic tension, at the same time sounding coherent and relevant.
sieben (G)	Seven.
sightreading	Playing a piece at first sight.
sightsinging	Singing a piece at first sight.

signal	In *synthesis*, an electronic impulse.
Signallampe (G)	Cue light.
signature	See *key signature*, *time signature*.
signature tune	A piece of music used by an entertainer or a dance band, to sign off a performance. The custom began in music hall, and continued into the early days of broadcasting, when it was used by dance bands.
silenzio (It)	Silence.
Simandl bow	Double bass bow, held with the palm up. See *Dragonetti*.
similar motion	*Part-writing* (or *voice-leading*) that runs in the same direction, up or down. As opposed to *contrary motion*.
simile, sim. (It)	Like, continue in the same manner.
simple interval	An interval of an octave or less. A larger interval is *compound*.
simplement (F)	Simply.
simple time,	A time signature in which the basic pulse
simple meter	is divisible by two. As opposed to *compound time*.
sin' (It)	Abbreviation of *sino*, 'until'.
sine wave	In *synthesis*, a pure symmetrical *waveform* that represents a simple sound with no *overtones*.
sinfonia (It)	**1.** *Symphony*.
	2. A small *orchestra*.
	3. An *overture*.
sinfonietta (It)	**1.** A short *symphony*.
	2. A small symphony orchestra.
Singakademie (G)	Singing academy. Title used by some choirs.
singbar (G)	Singable.
singend, singen (G)	Singing, to sing.
single	**1.** Term from the era of *vinyl* records, where a recording of two songs (one on each side of the *disc*) was issued.
	2. One who pursues a career as a soloist. (Jazz.)
single reed instrument	Instruments of the *clarinet* and *saxophone* families, which have one *reed* attached to (or originally fashioned from) a mouthpiece.
Singspiel (G)	A type of musical play where the musical numbers alternate with portions of dialogue.
sinistra (It)	Left (hand).
sino (It)	Until.
sistrum	An ancient percussion instrument, a Y-shaped frame with metal discs or rings threaded loosely on a rod that joins the two prongs of the Y.

sitar

An Indian form of the *lute*, with a long neck and moveable *frets*. It has from four to seven strings, and sometimes sympathetic strings.

sit in, sitting in

To play (briefly) with a band to which one does not normally belong.

Sitzprobe (G)

Rehearsal for singers.

six-four chord

A chord with the fifth in the bass. A second inversion *triad*. The name comes from the intervals above the bass, a sixth and a fourth.

sixteenth note

A note one sixteenth the duration of a whole note. *Semiquaver.*

sixth

A *diatonic* leap of six notes, including the first and last.

sixth chord

1. A chord with an added sixth.

2. A *triad* in first inversion. The name comes from the intervals above the bass, a sixth and a third.

sizzle cymbal

A large *cymbal* with loose fitting brass rivets inserted around the surface.

ska

A style of Jamaican pop music, a forerunner of *reggae.*

Skala (G)

Scale. Also *Tonleiter.*

skiffle

Style of music popular in the late 1950s in England, after the skiffle group led by Lonnie Donegan. A singer, accompanied by guitar (Sp), washboard and/or drums, bass (or a bass made from an old tea chest), and maybe a blown jug and harmonica.

skins

Slang for *drums.*

skip

Leap. As opposed to a *step.*

skirl, skirling

To shriek or sing shrilly. Adjective commonly used to describe the sound of *bagpipes.*

Skizze, Skizzen (G)

Sketch, sketches.

slam dancing

Violent dancing in which the dancers jump up and down and deliberately slam into each other.

slancio (It)

Impetus.

slap-bass

Originally a double bass *pizzicato* technique used in early dance bands and jazz. The string is plucked by being pulled out away from the instrument, and on release it clicks (or slaps) against the *fingerboard.* Later adapted most effectively for bass guitar.

slap stick

Part of what has been described as the 'rhythmic noise' department of the percussion section. Two thin pieces of flat wood, usually hinged, which are flapped together. Also called a *whip.*

slap-tonguing	A technique of *single reed wind instruments*. The tongue is pressed hard against the reed to create a vacuum between tongue and reed. When the tongue is pulled away sharply the release of the reed makes a percussive slap.
slargando, slentando (It)	Slowing up.
slått, slåtter (Norwegian)	Norwegian folk composition for the *Hardanger fiddle*.
slave	A device controlled or operated by another device.
sleigh-bell	Small spherical bell with slot-like mouth, traditionally attached to the harness of draft animals.
slide	**1.** *Glissando. Portamento.* A smooth glide from note to note.
	2. The moveable part of the *trombone* that alters the length of the air column.
slide guitar	An ordinary guitar that is played by using a *bottleneck* (a metal tube usually worn over the fifth finger of the chord hand), enabling the performer to slide between notes.
slider	The control of an electronic or electrical device that moves by sliding, e.g. a *fader*.
slide trumpet,	**1.** Slang name for the soprano trombone.
slide cornet	**2.** Small trumpet or cornet with valves played by the left hand, a slide operated by the right.
slip horn	Jazz slang for *trombone*. Also known as 'slush pump' and 'kid shifter'.
slit drum	Tropical percussion instrument. A log with slits.
slur	In notated music, a curved line connecting two or more notes.
smania (It)	Craze, frenzy.
smear	Jazz and dance band term for an exaggerated upward *glissando*, *slide* or *portamento*. The most famous exponent was Johnny Hodges, saxophonist in the Duke Ellington orchestra.
sminuendo, sminuito (It)	Diminishing, diminished.
smorendo (It)	Becoming softer and slower.
smorfioso (It)	Mincing.
smorzando, smorz. (It)	Fading away.
SMPTE	Society of Motion Picture and Television Engineers which, among other things, defines some technical standards.
snare	Usually an abbreviation of *snare drum*.

snare drum	A side drum, the most important item of the drum kit used in jazz and popular music. The snares are the multiple wire (formerly gut) strands which cross the underside of the drum and rattle against the skin.
snello, snellamente (It)	Nimble, nimbly.
so (G)	As.
soap opera	Not a musical term. A radio or television serial, named because of its popularity with soap manufacturers in commercial broadcasting.
soave, soavità (It)	Suave, suavely. Sweet, mild.
sock cymbal	*Hi-hat*. Two horizontal *cymbals* mounted face to face on a vertical shaft, and brought together by operating a foot pedal.
sofort (G)	Immediately.
soft pedal	The left pedal on the piano which, by various methods according to the size and type of instrument, softens the tone. See *una corda*.
soggetto (It)	*Subject*.
sogleich (G)	Immediately.
soh	In *tonic sol-fa* the name of the fifth degree of the scale.
sol	The note G, from which the *tonic sol-fa* name *soh* is derived.
sola (It)	Alone.
Soldatenzug (G)	Procession of soldiers.
solenne, solennemente, solennità (It)	Solemn, solemnly, solemnity.
solennel, solennelle (F)	Solemn.
sol-fa	See *tonic sol-fa*.
solfège (F), **solfeggio** (It)	A method of aural training and music-reading using names for each note of the melody.
soli (It)	Alone. Plural of *solo*.
solito (It)	Usual.
sollecitando (It)	Hastening forward.
sollecito (It)	Eager.
solmization	*Sightsinging* a passage, using the *sol-fa* syllables.
solo (It)	Alone. A piece for one instrument.
soltanto (It)	Solely.
sombre (F)	Dark, melancholy.
sommesso (It)	Subdued.
sommo, somma (It)	Highest. Utmost.
, sons (F)	Sound, sounds.

sonare (It)	To sound, to play.
sonata (It)	Sounded. Originally it was a piece played (sounded) as distinct from *cantata*, a piece sung. Since the time of Haydn and Mozart an instrumental work in three or four movements for one or two players.
sonata form	Also called first movement form, or compound *binary form*. The movement is divided into three sections, *exposition*, *development* and *recapitulation*. The key relationship between these sections is a significant aspect of sonata form.
Sonate (G)	*Sonata.*
sonatina (It), **sonatine** (F)	A little *sonata*.
sonevole (It)	Sonorous, resonant.
song	A piece for voice.
song cycle	A group of songs, usually with some unifying aspect.
songplugger	Employee of a music publisher who promoted songs to performers. Obsolete.
sonnerie (F)	Sounding.
sonoramente, sonoro (It)	Sonorously, sonorous.
sons bouchés (F)	Stopped notes in horn playing.
sopra (It)	Above.
Sopran (G)	*Soprano.*
sopranino (It)	Diminutive of *soprano*. Used for any instrument smaller (higher) than the soprano size, such as sopranino *recorder*, sopranino *saxophone*.
soprano (It)	'Upper'. 1. The highest type of female voice. 2. In a family of instruments, the name given to the one having a range similar to the soprano voice, e.g. soprano *saxophone*, soprano *flugelhorn*.
soprano clef	Little-used clef having middle C on the bottom line of the *staff*.
Sopransängerin (G)	(Female) soprano singer.
Sopranstimme (G)	Soprano voice, soprano part.
sorda, sordamente (It), **sordiniert** (G)	Subdued. Muffled.
sordino, sordini, sord. (It)	*Mute*, mutes.
sospirando, sospirante, sospirevole (It)	Sighing.
sostenendo, sostenente (It)	Sustaining.

sostenuto, sost. (It)	Sustained.
sotto (It)	Under.
sotto voce (It)	Under the voice.
soubrette (F)	Light soprano in *opera* or *operetta*.
soudainement (F)	Suddenly.
Souffleur (G)	Prompter.
Souffleurkasten (G)	Prompt box.
soufflieren (G)	To prompt.
soul music	Black pop music of the 1960s. Term later used to describe a type of *hard bop* jazz.
soundboard, sounding board	The board above which strings are stretched to give resonance, e.g. the belly of a guitar, or the board beneath the strings in a piano.
soundcheck	Rehearsal specifically for checking equipment and sound levels.
soundhole	The holes cut into the belly of a string instrument.
soundpost	In instruments of the *violin* family, the wooden post placed inside the instrument, between the belly and the back, and located beneath the *bridge*.
sound reinforcement	A general term for amplification. The term breaks the association with high volume levels that the word amplification creates.
sound system	A system for playing records, or amplifying speech, in public.
soupirant (F)	As if sighing.
sourd, sourde (F)	Muffled.
sourdine (F)	*Mute.*
sous (F)	Under.
sousaphone	A type of *tuba*, coiled to circle the player's body, with a high bell facing forwards above the player's head.
soutenu (F)	Sustained, *sostenuto.*
spandendo (It)	Expanding. Becoming more powerful.
Spanish guitar	Traditional classical guitar, with flat *belly* and back, single round *soundhole*, and six strings of gut or nylon.
spartito (It)	*Score.*
spasm band	An ensemble consisting mostly of simple or homemade instruments, such as *kazoo*, comb and paper, *washboard*, etc. Active in jazz before 1930.
Spass, spasshaft (G)	Joke, jocular.
spassapensieri (It)	*Jew's harp.*
speaker	Loudspeaker.

speaker key	A key in wind instruments that opens the hole which divides the wind column, and facilitates the playing of higher notes.
speaking trumpet	*Megaphone.*
species	Traditional method of teaching *counterpoint*, with five types (first species, second species, etc.) of increasing complexity.
spediendo (It)	Speeding.
speech-song	See *Sprechgesang*, *Sprechstimme*.
sperdendosi (It)	Fading out.
spezzato (It)	Divided.
spianato (It)	Smoothed out, smooth.
spiccato (It)	Demarcated. A string bowing technique in which the bow is bounced on the string.
spiegando (It)	Unfolding. Becoming louder.
Spiel (G)	Playing, performance.
spielen (G)	To act, to play.
Spieloper (G)	Comic opera.
spill	1. On wind instruments, a rapid downward run of notes (*chromatic* or *diatonic*). Used in *jazz* and *big band* styles. A *glissando* falling from the end of a note.
	2. The picking up - by a microphone - of sound from unwanted sources.
spinet	1. A small keyboard instrument, with an action similar to a *harpsichord*. See *Tafelklavier*.
	2. A small upright *piano*.
spinnen des Tons (G)	See *filar la voce*.
Spinnerlied, Spinnlied (G)	Spinner's song, spinning song.
spinto (It)	Pushed, urged on.
spirito, spiritoso (It)	Spirit, in a spirited manner.
spiritual	Religious folk song.
Spitze (G)	Point.
spitzig (G)	Pointed, cutting.
splash cymbal	A tiny, thin *cymbal*, between three and six inches in diameter, with a short, unsustained sound.
split point, split keyboard	A point on an electronic keyboard where a second playing area begins, having a separate sound.
spoons	Two domestic cutlery spoons used as a hand-held percussion instrument. The sound is produced by striking them against each other.

spöttisch (G)	Mocking.
Sprechchor (G)	Speech-choir. *Sprechgesang* applied chorally.
sprechend (G)	Speaking.
Sprechgesang (G)	Speech-song. Vocal style between song and speech. Used extensively by Arnold Schoenberg (1874-1951).
Sprechstimme (G)	Speech-voice. Voice using *Sprechgesang*.
springar (Norwegian)	Southern Norwegian folk dance for two people, in 3/4 time.
springdans (Norwegian)	Norwegian dance in 3/4 time.
springend (G)	Springing.
spugna, bacchetta di (It)	Sponge-headed drumstick.
square piano	Oblong piano, introduced in England in the mid-eighteenth century.
square wave	A synthesized *waveform* with a hollow timbre, similar to the sound of a *clarinet*.
squillante, squillanti (It)	'Clanging'. Instruction to percussionist to suspend *cymbals* and strike with sticks.
sringara	A deep-bodied Indian violin with a skin *belly*. It has three or four bowed strings, and a set of sympathetic strings.
SSA	Soprano, Soprano, Alto.
SSAA	Soprano, Soprano, Alto, Alto.
Staatskapelle (G)	State orchestra.
Staatsoper (G)	State opera house or company.
Stäbchen (G)	The beater for a *triangle*.
stabile (It)	Stable, firm, permanent, regular, resident.
stabs	Short percussive brass interjections in *big band* writing.
staccato, stacc. (It)	Detached.
Städtische Oper (G)	Municipal opera (house or company).
Stadtmusiker, Stadtpfeiferei (G)	(Municipal) street musicians.
staff, stave	The horizontal lines on which music is drawn.
stage band	*Big band.*
stage left	Prompt side. To the performer's left in Britain, to the right in USA.
stage monitor	Type of *foldback*. A floor-mounted loudspeaker provided onstage to enable a performer to hear details of the performance.
stage right	Opposite prompt side. To the performer's right in Britain, left in USA.
standard, standard tune	A popular song or Broadway tune that has become

a permanent part of the repertoire of jazz musicians and established middle-of-the-road (see *MOR*) performers. Many of the songs of Harold Arlen (Come Rain or Come Shine), Hoagy Carmichael (Georgia), Jerome Kern (All the Things You Are), Cole Porter (Just One of Those Things) and George Gershwin (I Got Rhythm) have become standards.

Ständchen (G) — *Serenade.*

standhaft, Standhaftigkeit (G) — Firm, firmness.

stark (G) — Strong, loud.

stark anblasen, stark blasend (G) — Blow strongly. An instruction to wind players.

Star-Spangled Banner — In a bill passed by the Senate in 1931, the official National Anthem of the USA. Prior to this date there was no official anthem, and this song shared the role with 'Hail Columbia' and 'My Country 'tis of Thee', the latter tune being that of *'God Save the Queen'*.

statt (G) — Instead of.

stave — *Staff.*

steel band — Ensemble of *steel drums* (*pans*).

steel drums — Drums (*pans*) made from oil barrels, the ends of the barrels being cut off, shaped (depressed) into pans, and indented to give specific pitches. Played with rubber-headed beaters. Developed in Trinidad in the 1930s and 1940s.

steel guitar — A type of (amplified) guitar placed horizontally on a frame, the pitch of the strings being controlled by sliding a steel bar along the strings rather than using the fingers. Also called *Hawaiian guitar.*

steel strings — Guitar or electric bass strings made from metal - not always steel. As opposed to gut or nylon.

Steg (G) — *Bridge* of a stringed instrument. *Am Steg* is the same as *sul ponticello*, play near the bridge.

Stehparterre (G) — Standing area, promenade area.

steigernd (G) — Increased, heightened.

Steinspiel (G) — *Stone chimes.*

Stellwerk (G) — Lighting control box.

stem — The vertical line connected to a note head.

stendendo (It) — Extending. Similar to *rallentando.*

stentare (It) — To labor.

step	Melodic movement of a second (one or two semitones).
step-time mode	The facility to be able to record electronically without having to play in real time, or even rhythmically.
sterbend (G)	Dying away.
stereo	Abbreviation of stereophonic, the effect of sound from different directions in three-dimensional space.
steso (It)	Extended, spreading out.
stesso, stessa (It)	The same.
stets (G)	Steadily. Always.
Stichwort (G)	Cue (speech).
stick	**1.** Everyday term for the wooden part of a string player's *bow*.
	2. *Baton.*
sticking	The hand patterns used by a drummer.
sticks	Instruction to a drummer to return to sticks after using some other beating device, such as *brushes*, *mallets* or bare hands.
Stierhorn (G)	Cow horn. Wagnerian instrument, often replaced by the *trombone.*
stile rappresentativo (It)	A term used by early seventeenth century Italian composers. Refers to the theater and the device of *recitative*, based on the natural spoken inflexions of the voice.
still (G)	Quiet, calm.
Stimme (G)	**1.** Voice.
	2. Vocal part.
Stimmführung (G)	*Voice leading. Part-writing.*
Stimmgabel (G)	*Tuning fork.*
Stimmung (G)	**1.** Tuning.
	2. Atmosphere, prevailing mood, ethos.
	3. Name of a 1968 work by Stockhausen.
Stimmzimmer (G)	Band room.
stinguendo (It)	Extinguishing, fading out.
stiracchiando, stiracchiato, stirando, stirato (It)	Slowing down, drawing out.
stochastic	Governed by the mathematical laws of probability. Device used by the Greek composer Iannis Xenakis (1922-2001).
stock arrangement,	An orchestration or band arrangement for

stock	a variable size of dance band or jazz ensemble, commercially produced and published.
stockend (G)	Coming to a standstill.
stomp	**1.** Probably derived from 'stamp'. Many early jazz pieces of a lively nature were called stomps, such as King Porter Stomp and Stompin' at the Savoy. **2.** 'To stomp' is to beat time vigorously with the foot.
stone chimes	Percussion instrument, with a short keyboard-like arrangement of tuned stone bars, struck by hand held beaters. Same as *Steinspiel*.
stop	**1.** A control on an *organ* that determines the amount of air supplied to a *register*. **2.** To depress the string on a string instrument. **3.** To insert hand into the bell of a horn.
stop chorus, stop time	A simple one (or two) measure pattern of sharp accents and rests, the rests usually predominating.
stornello (It)	Traditional Italian folk song, from Tuscany.
Strad	Abbreviation of Stradivarius, an instrument made by the violin maker Antonio Stradivari (1644-1737).
straff, straffer (G)	Strict, stricter. When applied to drumheads it means tight or tighter.
straight ahead	Conventional, straightforward, simple.
straight eighths	In theater music or jazz. Even eighth notes. Not swung.
straight mute	Conical hollow brass *mute*, usually made of cardboard or fiber.
strain	A musical section.
strascinando, strascinato (It)	Dragging, dragged.
Strat	Abbreviation of Stratocaster, a type of electric guitar made by the *Fender* company.
strathspey	A Scottish dance, a slower type of *reel*.
stravagante (It)	Extravagant. Fantastic.
straziante (It)	Tearing.
street piano	Mechanical piano, piano-organ. Operated by turning a handle, which actuates a mechanism similar to that of a *musical box*.
Streichinstrument (G)	String instrument.
Streichquartett (G)	*String quartet.*
streng (G)	Strict.
strepito, strepitoso (It)	Noise, noisy.

170

stretto (It)	Drawn together.
Strich (G)	A (bow) stroke.
stride	A piano style developed from *ragtime*. Named after the 'striding' effect of the left hand, leaping from a single bass note, on the first and third beats of the measure, to a middle-register chord on the second and fourth beats (the *backbeat*).
string bass	*Double bass, contrabass, bass fiddle, upright bass.*
stringendo (It)	Tightening. Increasing the tension, hurrying the tempo.
string quartet	Normally two *violins, viola, cello.*
string quintet	Normally two *violins,* two *violas, cello.*
strings	Instruments of the violin family. Stringed instruments.
string trio	*Violin, viola, cello.*
strisciando, strisciato (It)	Trailing, trailed. Smooth or slurred.
Strohfiedel (G)	*Xylophone.*
stroll	Cease to play.
stromento, stromenti (It)	See *strumento, strumenti.*
strophic	A song wherein all the verses use the same melody.
strum	To stroke the strings.
strumento, strumenti (It)	Instrument, instruments.
Stück (G)	Piece.
study	A piece written with some technical improvement as a goal.
study score	*Miniature score.*
stumm (G)	Silent, dumb.
stürmend, stürmisch (G)	Stormy, passionate.
su (It)	On.
subdominant	Fourth *degree* of the *diatonic* scale.
subito, sub. (It)	Suddenly.
subject	The theme as a basis for a musical development.
submediant	The sixth *degree* of the *diatonic* scale.
substitute chord	A reharmonization of a chord progression, where a *chromatic* chord replaces a *diatonic* chord.
subtone	Usually refers to the *clarinet* or *saxophone*. A style of quiet playing where the edge, power and much of the character is taken from the tone, but the pitch remains accurate. On the clarinet it is most effective in the low, *chalumeau*, register.
subtonic	The flattened seventh *degree* of the scale, e.g. B♭ in the key of C or C minor.
sugli, sui (It)	On the.

suite (F)	*Sequence.*
suite	A group of short instrumental pieces, usually dances, in the same key.
suivez (F)	Follow. (Instruction to accompanist.)
sul, sulla (It)	On the.
sul G, sul IV (It)	On the G, on the fourth (string). (Violin music.)
sul ponticello (It)	Bow on or next to the *bridge*.
sul tasto,	On the *fingerboard*.
sulla tastiera (It)	
summation tone	Same as *resultant tone*.
summen, summend (G)	To hum, humming.
suo (It)	Its own.
suo loco (It)	Its own place. Used, for example, after an instruction to play an octave higher or lower.
suono, suoni (It)	Sound, sounds.
supergroup	A rock group formed from the leading members of other groups.
supertonic	The *diatonic* note above the *tonic*. D in the key of C.
sur (F)	On, over.
surdo (P)	Drum played in *samba*, using a wooden stick with a velvet-covered head.
sur la touche (F)	On the *fingerboard*. Instruction to string players to bow on, or near to, the *fingerboard*.
sur le chevalet (F)	On the *bridge*. Instruction to string players to bow near to the bridge.
surtout (F)	Above all. Especially.
suspension	Where a *consonant* note is sustained whilst other voice or voices change, resulting in a *dissonance*, then resolved.
süss, süß (G)	Sweet.
sustain pedal	The right piano pedal, which raises the dampers. *Damper pedal.*
susurrando,	Whispering.
susurrante (It)	
svegliando, svegliato (It)	Awakening, awakened.
svelto (It)	Smart, quick.
swannee whistle	A simple whistle fitted with a slide to vary the length of the air column, and thus change the pitch. Mostly used as a toy, but sometimes employed as an effect in theater and broadcasting music. Used by Ravel in *L'Enfant et les sortilèges*.
sweet potato	*Ocarina.*

swell pedal	A foot-operated (or sometimes knee-operated) control on electronic instruments, to adjust volume.
swing	A forward-moving quality that is exhibited by jazz performances, but which resists definition.
swing era	Period in jazz from the mid-thirties to the early mid-forties when American jazz, particularly the big bands of Benny Goodman, Glen Miller, Artie Shaw, Count Basie and Duke Ellington, provided the pop music of the day.
switch, musical	A light music arrangement which consists of a medley of many short items, which change unexpectedly and without warning or preparation, thus 'switching' between familiar tunes.
sword dance	A dance performed sword in hand, or among or over swords.
sympathetic string	A string that vibrates in response to other sounds, without being touched.
symphonia	Greek word used to replace *symphony*.
symphonic band, symphonic wind band	*Concert band, military band.*
symphonic poem	Term introduced by Franz Liszt (1811-1886) to describe a work of symphonic proportions, but with an extra-musical interpretation.
symphonie (F)	*Symphony.*
symphonique (F), **symphonisch** (G)	Symphonic.
symphonische Dichtung (G)	*Symphonic poem.*
symphony	Sounding together. A serious and substantial orchestral work.
syncopation	An effect of rhythmic displacement by emphasizing weak beats or weaker parts of beats.
Synkope (G)	*Syncopation.*
synthesis, synthesize	To put together. Electronic sound manipulation.
synthesizer	Electronic device capable of generating and processing a variety of sounds.
syrinx	*Panpipes.*
system	In musical notation, two or more *staves* connected together.
System (G)	*Stave.*
Szene (G)	Scene.

T

t	*Tonic sol-fa* symbol for the seventh *degree* of the scale, the *leading note*.
t	Guitar *tablature* instruction to tap with strumming hand.
tabla	Indian hand drum with three skins on the head. Wooden, conical in shape, played in pairs.
tablature	A diagramatic notation which eventually gave way to the first versions of the notation in use today. Tablature survives as a system for instruments such as *lute, guitar, ukulele, banjo,* and *mandolin* - the fretted string instruments. It shows left hand finger positions, using lines for strings, and numbers (or letters) for frets.
table music	See *Tafelmusik.*
tabor	The earliest form of *snare drum.*
tabs	Curtains in the theater. Sometimes the title of the piece that is to be played as curtain music, for bows and applause.
Tabulatur (G)	*Tablature.*
tacere (It)	To be silent.
tacet, tacent (L)	Be silent. Instruction to performers, in written music.
tactus (L)	The measurement of the length of a beat, used in the fifteenth century, prior to the invention of *bar lines*.
Tafelklavier (G)	Table keyboard. *Virginal* or *spinet*.
Tafelmusik (G)	Table music. Music for social occasions, particularly at dinner or a banquet.
tag, tag ending	The ending or *coda* of a piece, often characterized by an *interrupted cadence*. For example, in the key of C, the music may arrive at G7 as the (expected) penultimate chord, and be 'interrupted' by an A7 chord. This is the beginning of the tag; the harmonies then return to the original key cyclically. Or are interrupted by a tag…
tailgate	Style of trombone playing used in New Orleans jazz. Early bands played in the street, transported by wagons. Trombonists needed room to manipulate their slides, and so stood to play at the wagon's tailgate.

take	A single recording made in a studio. Also used as a verb, e.g. 'to take', meaning 'to record'.
Takt (G)	1. Bar, measure.
	2. Meter, time, beat.
im Takt	In strict time.
taktmäßig (G)	In time.
Taktmesser (G)	*Metronome.*
Taktschlag (G)	Beat.
Taktstock (G)	*Baton.*
Taktstrich (G)	*Bar line.*
Taktzeichen (G)	*Time signature.*
tala	System of rhythmic or metrical cycles in Indian music. Also **taal**, **thal**, **tal**. Different ways of dividing a unit of time into a number of percussive beats.
talkback	Facility to allow a recording engineer in a control room to speak to musicians in the studio.
talking drum	West African drum, used for communication, wherein the pitch is adjusted by altering the tension of the lacing. The drum has a waisted shape, and is beaten with a curved stick.
talon (F)	*Heel.* The heel or *nut* of the *bow* of a stringed instrument. The end held by the player.
tamborim (P)	Small *tambourine*, without *jingles*, played with a stick.
Tambour (G)	Military drummer.
tambour (F), tambor (P)	*Drum.*
tambour de Basque (F)	*Tambourine.*
tambourin (F)	*Tabor.*
tambourine	Percussion instrument, small hand-held circular frame (with or without a head), with *jingles*.
tambour militaire (F)	*Side drum.*
tambur, tambura	Long-necked round-bodied *lute,* with four strings and no frets.
Tamburin (G)	*Tambourine.*
tamburo (It)	*Drum.*
tampon (F)	Drumstick.
tam-tam	A large *gong.*
tändelnd (G)	Playfully.
tangent	The brass blade (or tongue) in the mechanism of the *clavichord* that both presses the string and determines the pitch of the note.
tango (Sp)	An Argentinian dance.

tan-tan (P)	A deep drum similar to an *atabaque*.
tanto (It)	Much, so much.
Tanz, Tänze (G)	Dance, dances.
tap-dancing	Dancing with tapping of the feet.
tapping-on	A percussive effect on the *guitar* and *bass guitar*, obtained by *hammering-on* the string with the plectrum hand.
tar	Instrument used to accompany Ashough songs. See also *duduk, kamancha, kanon*.
tarantella (It), **tarantelle** (F)	A dance in fast 6/8 time, named after the Italian town of Taranto. The dance is traditionally connected with tarantism, a type of hysteria believed (wrongly) to be caused by the bite of the tarantula spider.
tardando (It)	Becoming slower.
tardo, tarda, tardamente (It)	Slow, slowly.
tárogató	Hungarian single reed woodwind instrument with a conical bore.
tarol (P)	Brazilian shallow two-headed drum with strings across skin (snares). Played with sticks.
Tastatur, Taste, Tasten (G)	*Keyboard*, key, keys - of a keyboard instrument.
tasto (It)	1. Key of a *keyboard*.
	2. *Fingerboard* or *fretboard*.
tattoo	Music of *bugles* and *drums*. Nowadays a spectacle in its own right, but also functional when used to recall soldiers to their barracks at night.
technischer Direktor (G)	Technical director.
technischer Leiter (G)	Stage director.
teclados (P)	Keyboards.
tedesco, tedesca (It)	German.
Te Deum (L)	Te Deum laudamus, We Praise Thee God. A hymn of praise.
teenybopper	A young *pop* fan.
Teil (G)	Part.
tema (It)	Theme.
temperament	The adjustment in size of musical intervals away from perfection to achieve an *octave* divided into twelve semitones of equal size, hence *equal temperament*.
tempestoso, tempestosamente (It)	Tempestuous, tempestuously.

176

temple bells	Large suspended bells, from the Far East. Struck with a horizontal wooden beam hung on ropes, or a mallet.
temple block	A hollowed wooden block, usually spheroid in shape, made in several sizes, customarily painted in red and gold, and played with a stick.
tempo (It)	Time. Pace.
tempo primo (It)	At the same *tempo* as at first.
tempo wie vorher (G)	Time as before.
temps (F)	Beat.
ten.	**1.** Abbreviation for *tenuto*.
	2. Abbreviation for *tenor*.
tendre, tendrement (F)	Tender, tenderly.
tenendo (It)	Sustaining.
teneramente, tenero (It)	Tenderly, tender.
tenerezza (It)	Tenderness.
tenor	**1.** The highest normal male voice.
	2. Descriptive term for instruments in the tenor range.
	3. Abbreviation for *tenor saxophone*.
tenor banjo	A version of the *banjo* using four strings, usually with violin tuning.
tenor clef	A *clef* on which the note middle C is written on the fourth (i.e. top-but-one) line of the staff. Sometimes used for *cello, double bass, bassoon* and *tenor trombone*.
tenor cor	A version of the *French horn*, a type of *saxhorn*.
tenor drum	A drum of type similar to the *snare drum*, but slightly larger and deeper, and without snares.
tenor horn	A type of *saxhorn*, with the bell held upwards.
tenoroon	A small *bassoon*, now obsolete, a fourth or fifth higher than the ordinary instrument. *Basson quinte* in French.
tenor saxophone	See *saxophone*.
Tenorschlüssel (G)	*Tenor clef.*
tenor trombone	See *trombone*.
tenth	An interval of an octave and a third. An interval containing ten note letter names, including the first and last notes.
tenuto, ten. (It)	**1.** Held. Hold a note for its full value, or sometimes longer.
	2. The tenuto symbol is a horizontal line placed above a note head.

terminal vibrato (jazz)	*Vibrato* placed at the very end of a long note, mostly used by wind instruments.
ternary form	In three sections, ABA, or AABA.
territory band	American term used in the 1920s and 1930s to describe dance bands and jazz bands that were based in a regional capital, but made extensive tours of the outlying area.
tertian harmony, **tertiary harmony**	Harmony built up in thirds, as opposed to *quartal harmony*, which is harmony built from intervals of fourths.
Terz (G)	Third.
tessitura (It)	Literally 'texture'. The compass wherein a singer's voice naturally lies. The general span of a vocal part, e.g. 'high tessitura', 'low tessitura'. Not the same as *range*.
testa (It)	Head. *Voce di testa*, 'head voice'.
testo (It)	Text, *libretto*.
tetrachord	Four note scale. The scale of C major has two tetrachords, C to F, and G to C.
texture	The number of parts and the way in which they are used. Relative density.
Theater (G)	Theater.
Theaterkasse (G)	Box office.
theater organ	See *cinema organ*.
Theaterstück (G)	Play (theatrical).
Thema (G)	Theme, subject.
theme	Musical subject, or the extramusical idea behind a piece.
theme and variations	A statement of a musical subject, followed by variations (development) on that subject or its harmonies.
theme song	See *signature tune*.
Theorbe (G)	*Theorbo*.
theorbo	A type of bass lute (*archlute*) with long extra strings.
Thérémin	Electronic musical instrument invented by Léon Thérémin in the 1920s. Similar to the later *Ondes Martenot*.
thesis (Greek)	Downbeat, downstroke, or strong beat.
third	Three steps in the major or minor scale, counting the top and bottom notes.
third inversion	A seventh chord with the seventh note in the bass.
Third Stream	A term coined by the musician and writer Gunther

Schuller, during a lecture at Brandeis University, USA, in 1957. It was originally a term to describe a style that fused basic elements of jazz and Western art music - a third stream.

thoroughbass — *Basso continuo.*

thrash metal — Pop music derived from *heavy metal.*

through-composed — Song in which the music for each stanza is different, as opposed to *strophic.*

thumb line — An inner line in the harmony, so-called because on the piano it can be taken by the thumb.

thumb piano — Set of small metal strips mounted on a hand-held resonator box. Played with the thumbs. *Mbira.*

thumb string — The banjo string that carries the melody. Can be any string, but played with the thumb.

thunder machine — A piece of theatrical equipment that imitates thunder. Frequently no more than a very large sheet of metal fitted with a handle by which it can be shaken to produce a rumble.

thunder stick — Flat blade attached to a cord, whirled to produce a whirring sound. Also *bullroarer* and *whizzer.*

tie — A curved line connecting two notes of the same pitch. The second note is not to be struck afresh.

tief (G) — Deep, flat, low.

tiefgespannt (G) — Deep-stretched. Refers to a drum that is loosely tuned, to give a low sound.

tierce de Picardie (F) — *Picardy third.* The ending of a minor key piece with a major chord. Unfortunately the origin of the naming of the term is unknown.

till ready — Direction (to accompanist) to play a short section repeatedly until receiving the *cue* to move on.

timbale, timbales — 1. *Kettledrum.*
2. Latin American drums, usually a pair mounted on a stand, and played with sticks.

timbre (F) — Stamp. An individual mark. Tone quality.

timbrel — Old English for *tambourine.*

time — Simple, regular pulse in jazz, as in the instruction 'play time'.

time signature — The numbers at the start of a piece, the lower figure conveying the kind of beats in the measure, and above this how many such beats.

timido, timidezza (It) — Timid, timidity.

timing clock — A synthesizer synchronizing code, for *MIDI.*

timore (It) — Fear.

timpani (It)	*Kettledrums*. The spelling *tympani* is incorrect.
tine	The metal tuning fork that produces the note on electric pianos.
tin mute	*Harmon mute.*
Tin Pan Alley	Name for the areas of London (Denmark Street, off Charing Cross Road) and New York (around 28ᵗʰ Street in Manhattan) where sheet music publishers used to have their offices.
tinter, tintement (F)	To tinkle, tinkling.
tintinnare (It)	To tinkle.
tinto (It)	Color.
tin whistle	An end-blown six-hole metal flute, with no keys. Sometimes called *penny whistle*.
tirana (Sp)	A Spanish dance-song, Andalusian in origin.
tirer, tiré (F)	To draw, drawn. Bowing instruction, implying down-bow.
tirolese (It)	Tyrolese.
toada (P)	Type of Brazilian song.
tobend (G)	Blustering.
toccata (It)	Touched. Usually a composition for keyboard instruments, featuring fast scales and arpeggios.
todt (G)	Dead. An archaic spelling. Now spelt *'tot'*.
toile (F)	Curtain. Theater term. See also *tabs*.
tome (F)	Volume.
tom-tom	**1.** As part of the dance band or jazz kit, a floor mounted single-headed deep drum. **2.** A barrel-shaped double-headed drum, tuned by moving rings up and down the lacing holding the threads.
Ton, Töne (plural) (G)	**1.** Sound. **2.** Tone. **3.** Note.
ton (F)	**1.** Pitch. **2.** Key. **3.** Tone. **4.** *Crook.* **5.** Sound.
tonada (Sp)	'Tune', air.
tonadilla (Sp)	Type of Spanish stage entertainment, with singing.
tonal	Having a key or mode. As opposed to *atonal*. A modified *answer* in a *fugue*.
Tonalität (G)	*Tonality.*
tonality	Having a key, or *tonic* note, as opposed to *atonality*.

tonante (It)	Thunderous.
Tonart (G)	Key.
Tonband (G)	Tape. (Reel.)
Tonbandaufnahme (G)	Tape recording.
Tondichter (G)	Composer. 'Tone poet'.
Tondichtung (G)	Composition. Tone poem. *Symphonic poem.*
tondo (It)	'Round'. Full-toned.
tone	1. A note.
	2. Quality of a musical sound. Tone color.
	3. The interval of two semitones; a second.
tonebars	*Drawbars.*
tonecluster	A group of adjacent notes played simultaneously. On a keyboard these may be played with the flat or side of the hand, or with the forearm.
tone poem	*Symphonic poem.* A translation of the German term *Tondichtung.*
tone row	In *dodecaphonic* (*serial* or *twelve-tone*) music, the order of the twelve notes.
tone-wheel	In early electric organs, the spinning disc that generates the sound electromagnetically.
tonguing	On wind instruments, starting and stopping the note with the tongue. *Articulation.*
tonic	The keynote, the first degree of the scale.
tonic sol-fa	An English notation and sight-singing system invented by Miss S.A. Glover in the nineteenth century and developed and popularized by John Curwen (1816-1880). Using a *movable doh*, the names for the seven steps of the major scale are doh, ray, me, fah, soh, lah, te.
tonitruone (It)	*Thunder machine.* A sheet of metal fitted with handles, shaken to produce the sound of thunder.
Tonkunst (G)	Knowledge of music. 'Tone-art'.
Tonkünstler (G)	Composer. 'Tone-artist'.
Tonleiter (G)	*Scale.*
tonlos (G)	Toneless.
tonnerre (F)	Thunder.
tono (It)	1. *Tone.*
	2. Key, pitch.
	3. Thunder.
Tonreihe (G)	Note row, *tone row.*
Tonsetzer (G)	Composer. 'Note setter'.
Tonstufe (G)	Register.
top line	Melody. Highest voice.

torch song	An emotional and poignant rendering of a popular song, in the theater or in cabaret. The origins of the description lie in the phrase 'carrying a torch for someone', i.e. suffering the pain of unrequited love.
tornare, tornando (It)	To return, returning.
tosto (It)	Quick.
tot (G)	Modern spelling of *todt*, 'dead'.
Totentanz (G)	Dance of death.
touch	The manner in which a performer's fingers manipulate the keyboard.
touche (F)	**1.** A key of a keyboard instrument. **2.** A *fret*. **3.** The *fingerboard*.
touch sensitivity	Mechanism linked to synthesizer keys to enable other parameters to be controlled. Also called *velocity sensitivity*.
toujours (F)	Always.
Tourte bow	The type of modern *bow* in general use for all members of the *violin* family, named after the inventor François Tourte (1747-1835).
tout à coup (F)	Suddenly.
tout à fait (F)	Completely.
tout de suite (F)	Immediately.
track	**1.** One of the invisible stripes of sound on a magnetic tape. **2.** A section of a *vinyl* record, *cassette* or *CD*, containing one musical item.
tracker action	Version of organ mechanism, having a direct mechanical link between the key and the pipe, as opposed to electronic or pneumatic links.
trad	Abbreviation of *traditional jazz*.
trading fours	In jazz performances, when soloists play alternate four measure improvised passages.
traditional jazz	Term originally used to describe New Orleans jazz, probably coined during the post-Second World War revival. Now frequently used to describe any jazz pre-fusion.
tradotto (It), **traduit** (F)	**1.** Translated. **2.** Arranged. **3.** Transposed.
traduzione (It), **traduction** (F)	**1.** Translation. **2.** Arrangement. **3.** *Transposition*.

Tragödie, Trauerspiel (G)	Tragedy.
tramline	Slang for the pair of parallel lines denoting a sudden break in the music. *Caesura.*
tranquillo (It)	Calm.
transcribe, transcription	To write out. To write down an improvised passage. Frequently and incorrectly used in reference to sound recordings made from a live broadcast. Sometimes used, incorrectly, as a synonym for *arrangement.*
transition	A brief passing *modulation.*
transponieren (G)	To *transpose.*
transpose, transposition	The act of writing or playing music in a different key from the original.
transposing instruments	Instruments which do not play at the pitch of their notation. Thus when a clarinet in B♭ plays a written C, it will sound B♭, a tone lower. A saxophone in E♭ playing a written C will sound E♭, a sixth lower. Music for the B♭ clarinet or E♭ saxophone (and for all other transposing instruments) has to be *transposed* into the appropriate key.
transverse flute	*Flute* in which the air stream is directed over the embouchure hole in a direction **across** the body of the instrument, as opposed to end-blown.
traps, trap set	Old dance band and jazz term for the *kit* played by a kit drummer.
trascinando (It)	Dragging. Same as *rallentando.*
Trauer (G)	Mourning, sorrow.
Trauermarsch (G)	Funeral march.
Trauermusik (G)	Funeral music.
traurig (G)	Sad.
tre (It)	Three.
treble	The highest voice in choral singing.
treble clef	The G clef, encircling the second line of the staff.
tre corde (It)	Three strings. In piano music, indicates the release of the left or 'soft' pedal, allowing all the strings of a note to vibrate.
tremolo, trem. (It)	With tremolo. Tremolo is Italian for trembling. Strictly, tremolo is a rapid fluctuation of the amplitude of a sound. *Vibrato* is the fluctuation of pitch.
tremolo arm	Lever fixed to a guitar which changes the pitch of

183

	the strings by moving the *bridge*. Also called *whammy bar*, or *vibrola*.
tremulant	Name of a *stop* on a pipe organ, which produces rapid fluctuations in the wind supply.
trenodia (It)	Threnody, *dirge*.
trepak	Russian dance.
très (F)	Very.
triad	A three note chord, root, third and fifth.
triangle	Small three-cornered percussion instrument made from a steel bar, played with a steel rod or a drumstick.
triângulo (P)	*Triangle.*
trigger	A pulsed voltage of very short duration used to control an electronic device such as a *drumpad*.
trill	Rapid alternation of the written note and the note above. *Shake.*
Triller (G)	*Trill.*
Triller mit Nachschlag (G)	*Trill* with *turn*
Triller ohne Nachschlag (G)	*Trill* without *turn.*
trillo (It)	1. *Trill.* 2. Seventeeth century vocal ornament in which a single note is repeated, the repetitions increasing in speed.
Trinklied (G)	Drinking song.
trio	1. An ensemble of three performers. 2. A piece for three performers. 3. The central section of a *minuet*, called trio because it was originally written for three instruments. See *trio sonata*.
Triole (G), **triolet** (F)	*Triplet.*
trionfale, trionfante (It)	Triumphant.
trio sonata	A *Baroque* form of *chamber music*, usually with two melodic instruments (e.g. two violins) and continuo (e.g. cello and a keyboard instrument). Thus, it is actually played by four performers!
triple concerto	*Concerto* with three soloists.
triple counterpoint	Simultaneous combination of three melodies or voices, which can be interchanged.
triplet	A group of three notes of equal value, written where a group of two or four is suggested by the time signature.

triplet feel	An instruction to play pairs of eighth notes with a swung feel, long-short, approximating to twelve eight.
triple tonguing	Fast tonguing on wind instruments using both forward and backward (or upward and downward) strokes of the tongue.
triste (F), (It), **tristemente** (It)	Sad, sadly.
tristesse (F), **tristezza** (It)	Sadness.
tritone	Interval of three tones. The augmented fourth or diminished fifth.
tritone substitution	The two most important notes of a dominant seventh chord, the third and the seventh, (B and F in the chord of G7), form a tritone with each other. These two notes, B and F, belong to one other dominant seventh, D♭7. Thus, tritone substitution replaces G7 by D♭7, introducing chromatic color to the music.
trois (F)	Three.
tromba (It)	*Trumpet.*
tromba a macchina, **tromba cromatica** (It)	Valve trumpet.
tromba marina (It)	Marine trumpet. An obsolete bowed instrument.
trombone	Literally, 'large trumpet'. Tenor brass instrument, normally played with a *slide*, though a *valve* version exists.
trombonino (It)	*Alto trombone.*
Trommel (G)	*Drum.*
grosse Trommel (G)	*Bass drum.*
kleine Trommel (G)	*Side drum.*
Rührtrommel (G)	*Tenor drum.*
Trompete (G), **trompette** (F)	*Trumpet.*
trop (F), **troppo** (It)	Too much.
trope	Music introduced into *plainsong*.
troubadour	An eleventh to thirteenth century wandering poet musician (*minstrel*) of southern France. Literally 'inventor' or 'finder' in Provençal. See *trouvère*.
trouvère (F)	Northern French equivalent of *troubadour*.
trüb, trübe (G)	Gloomy, sad.
Trugschluß (G)	*Interrupted cadence.*
trumpet	Member of the brass family, the modern form having a cylindrical bore, flared bell, cup-shaped mouthpiece and three valves.

trumpet marine	Obsolete bowed instrument.
truss rod	A metal rod set lengthways into the neck of a guitar to prevent the neck from bending due to the tension of the strings.
tsigane, tzigane (F)	Gypsy. As German *Zigeuner*.
Tsugaru-jamisen	Northern Japanese three-string *lute*.
TTB	Tenor, Tenor, **B**ass (or **B**aritone).
TTBB	Tenor, Tenor, **B**ass, **B**ass (or **B**aritone).
tuba	Large brass instrument made in several sizes and shapes. Has a curved conical bore and a flared bell.
tube	American for *valve*, an electronic device now largely replaced by the integrated circuit (IC).
tube out	Instruction to *trumpet* player to remove the stem from the *Harmon* mute.
Tubist, Tubaspieler (G)	*Tuba* player.
tubo di ricambio (It)	Changing tube. The *crook* or *shank* of a brass instrument.
tubs	Jazz slang for drums.
tubular bells, tubular chimes	A set of tuned steel tubes suspended from a frame and played with beaters or mallets.
tucket	Obsolete Shakespearian word for a *fanfare*.
tune	1. To adjust the pitch of an instrument. 2. Melody.
tuner	Person who adjusts the pitch of instruments.
tuning	The act of adjusting the pitch of an instrument.
tuning fork	A two-tined metal object constructed accurately to sound the exact pitch of a note when struck.
tuono, tono (It)	1. *Tone.* 2. *Mode.* 3. *Key.* 4. Thunder.
turba (L)	Crowd. Refers to words spoken or uttered during *Passion* music.
turca, alla (It)	In the Turkish style.
turkey trot	Early twentieth century American dance, associated with *ragtime*.
Türkisch (G)	Turkish.
Turkish crescent	A long stick bearing a tent-shaped or hat-shaped construction, and a crescent-shaped plate further down the stick. Small bells are attached, and are sounded by shaking the instrument. Also known as Turkish jingle, *Chinese pavilion, pavillon chinois, jingling Johnny* and *Schellenbaum*.

turn	An ornament of four or five notes that make a turn around a note.
turnround, turnaround,	The measures leading up to the repeat.
turnback	The halfway *cadence*. Commonly labelled first time bar, second time bar, etc. Norwegian musicians call these bars first house, second house, etc.
turque (F)	Turkish.
Tusch (G)	A *fanfare*.
tutto, tutti (It)	All.
twelfth	Interval of an *octave* plus a *fifth*.
twelve bar blues	Traditional twelve measure (bar) cyclic form of the blues, and of much early rock 'n' roll. The simpler forms use only the *primary chords* (I, IV and V). There is a variety of progressions used, but all move to the subdominant at measure five.
twelve-note	*Serial*, or *dodecaphonic*.
twelve-string guitar	A guitar where the strings are in unison pairs. That is, six double strings, making twelve in all.
twelve-tone scale	*Note row. Tone row. Dodecaphonic scale.*
twelve-tone technique	The technique of writing *serial, twelve-tone* or *twelve-note* music. *Dodecaphony.*
twist	Popular dance of the 1960s.
two-beat	A feel induced by emphasizing the first and third beats of music in four-four, i.e. the bass plays two in a measure. This came to jazz and popular music from the European march, by way of *ragtime*.
two-part form	*Binary* form.
twos	Two measure phrases.
two-step	A gliding dance in duple time.
tympani	Misspelling of *timpani*.
tzigane (F)	*Tsigane.*

U

üben (G)	To practice.
über (G)	Over, above.
Übergang (G)	Transition.
übergreifen (G)	To overlap, cross hands.
übermässig,	Augmented.
übermäßig (G)	
übermütig (G)	High-spirited.
Übung (G)	Exercise, practice.
ud	*Oud.*
uguale (It)	Equal, exactly the same.
ukulele, (ukelele)	Small four-string *guitar* from Hawaii, but of Portuguese origin. Not to be confused with the *Hawaiian guitar.*
ultimo, ultima (It)	Last.
Umkehrung (G)	*Inversion.*
Umkehrung des	*Retrograde* inversion (in serialism).
Krebses (G)	
umstimmen (G)	To change the usual tuning.
Umwendung (G)	*Inversion.*
una corda (It)	One string. See *soft pedal.*
unbestimmt (G)	Indefinite.
und (G)	And.
ungar, ungarisch (G)	Hungarian.
ungeduldig (G)	Impatient.
ungefähr (G)	Approximate.
ungherese (It)	Hungarian.
unhörbar (G)	Silent.
unison	Several instruments or voices playing or singing the same note.
unisono, unis. (It)	*Unison.*
unmerklich (G)	Imperceptible.
uno, una (It)	A, one.
un peu (F)	A little.
un poco (It)	A little.
unruhig (G)	Restless.
unten (G)	Below, underneath.
unter (G)	Under, lower.
Unterdominante (G)	*Subdominant.*
Untermediante (G)	*Submediant.*
Unterricht (G)	Instruction, lesson, teaching.

upbeat	**1.** *Pickup, anacrusis.* **2.** Optimistic, lively, up-tempo. **3.** Unaccented beat, *backbeat*, beat two or four in *common time*.
up-bow	Bowing a string instrument away from the player.
upper partial	A constituent of the *harmonic series*.
upright bass	A conventional, traditional acoustic *double bass*, as opposed to a solid-bodied amplified *bass guitar*.
upright piano	A piano in which the strings and soundboard are vertical, as opposed to the horizonal configuration of the grand piano.
upstage	**1.** The part of the stage away from the audience. **2.** To outdo someone, or out-perform them. Comes from the hostile theatrical practice of acting on the upstage side of a fellow Thespian, thus obliging the victim to face away from the audience to deliver lines.
up-tempo	Fast.
Uraufführung (G)	First performance, première.
ursprünglich (G)	Original.
Urtext (G)	Pure original text, without editing.
ut (F)	The note C.
ut supra (L)	As before, as above.

V

v — Guitar *tablature* for *vibrato*.

va (It) — Go on, continue.

vacillando (It), **vacillant** (F) — Wavering. Refers to string instrument *vibrato*.

vaghezza (It) — 1. Longing. 2. Grace, charm.

vago (It) — Vague.

valeur (F) — Value.

valse (F) — *Waltz*.

valve — 1. British term for electronic *tube*. Now largely replaced by integrated circuits (ICs). 2. Mechanism on brass instruments which diverts the air around different lengths of tubing.

valve instruments — Brass instruments where the length of tube is altered mechanically by use of valves.

valve trombone — *Trombone*, operated by valves instead of a *slide*. *Cimbasso*.

vamp — A short repetitive *introduction* (usually improvised) played by an accompanist.

vamp till ready — Instruction to accompanist to fill time by playing a repetitive *introduction*.

vaporeux, vaporeuse (F) — Vaporous.

variable — In *synthesis*, any parameter that can be altered.

variante (F), (It) — Variant.

variation — A passage of music which develops or varies a given theme.

variazione, variazioni (It) — Variation, variations.

varié (F) — Varied.

vaudeville — 1. In eighteenth century France, a popular, satirical or topical song. 2. A show with music, dancing and comedy. In Britain known as a variety show, or variety.

VCA — Voltage Controlled Amplifier. In *synthesis*, the device that controls the level of a signal in proportion to the level of a controlling voltage.

VCF — Voltage Controlled Filter. In *synthesis*, the device that controls the harmonic content of a signal in proportion to the level of a controlling voltage.

VCO — Voltage Controlled Oscillator. In *synthesis*, the

VDU

veemente (It)

velato (It)

velocemente, veloce (It)

velocity

velocity sensitivity

Venetian School

vent (F)

Ventil (G), **ventile** (It)

Ventilposaune (G)

Ventiltrompete (G)

verbunko

verdoppeln (G)

Verein (G)

Verfolger (G)

verhallend (G)

verismo (It)

Verklärte Nacht (G)

verkleinert (G)

verklingen,
verlöschen (G)

verliebt (G)

verlierend (G)

vermindert (G)

verminderter
   Dreiklang (G)

Verschiebung (G)

verschwindend (G)

verse

device that controls the frequency of a signal in proportion to the level of a controlling voltage.

Visual Display Unit. A television monitor.

Vehement.

Veiled.

Quickly, quick.

In *synthesis*, the *MIDI* code that transmits dynamics.

In *synthesis*, the ability to respond to how quickly a key is pressed or how hard it is struck.

A group of composers in Venice in the late *Renaissance* period. Their style contains the beginnings of *orchestration* and *polychoral* textures.

Wind.

Valve.

Valve trombone.

Valve trumpet.

A lively Hungarian dance associated with the recruitment of soldiers.

To double.

Society.

Follow spot. (Moving spotlight.)

Fading away.

Realism. A late-romantic style of Italian opera that emphasized realistic plots.

Transfigured Night. Work by Schoenberg, opus 4, (1899).

Diminished.

To die away.

In love. To be freshly in love.

Losing itself. Dying away.

Diminished.

Diminished triad.

A displacing. Using the *soft pedal* of the piano.

Disappearing.

1. The solo portion of an *anthem*.

2. In popular song, the scene-setting anticipatory section, before the chorus.

3. In popular song, the stanza which tells the story, changing with each repeat.

Versenkung (G)	Trap (stage).
verset (F)	A short organ piece.
versetzen (G)	To transpose.
Versetzung (G)	*Transposition.*
Versetzungszeichen (G)	*Accidental* sign.
verstärken (G)	To strengthen.
verstimmt (G)	Out of tune.
verteilt, vertheilt (G)	Divided, spread out.
vertonen (G)	To set to music.
Vertrag (G)	Contract.
verweilend (G)	Delaying. *Rallentando.*
Verzeichnis (G)	Index. Catalog.
Verzierungen (G)	Embellishments.
Vespers	The evening church service.
via (It)	Away!
vib.	Abbreviation of *vibrato.*
vibes	*Vibraphone.*
vibraphone, vibraharp	Percussion instrument with tuned metal bars laid out in the pattern of a piano keyboard. These are played with beaters. There is a sustaining mechanism, and electrically driven fans produce a *vibrato* effect.
vibraslap	Percussion instrument.
vibrato (It)	A small repeated fluctuation in pitch used by instrumentalists and singers. Can also be programmed into a synthesizer. Widely used, but not so widely noticed by listeners - to the extent that some critics and students frequently state, 'so and-so doesn't use vibrato', when this is plainly untrue to those who listen carefully.
vibrer (F)	To vibrate.
vibrola	*Whammy bar.*
vicino (It)	Near.
vide (F)	Empty. Open.
vide (L)	See. Instruction in a manuscript score to make a performance cut.
viel (G)	Much, plenty, a lot of.
vielle (F)	*Hurdy-gurdy*, or alternatively a flat-backed medieval violin, precursor of the *viol*, with one of the three to five strings being a drone.
vier (G)	Four.
vierfach (G)	Fourfold.
vierhändig (G)	Four-handed. For four hands, i.e. a piano *duet.*

192

Vierte (G)	Fourth.
Viertel (G)	Quarter. *Quarter note, crotchet.*
vif, vive (F)	Lively.
vigueur, vigoureux,	Vigor, vigorous, vigorously.
vigoureusement (F),	
vigore, vigoroso,	
vigorosamente (It)	
vihuela	A six-string Spanish *Renaissance* instrument, with guitar shape.
villancico	**1.** Spanish poetical and musical song-form. **2.** An extended *cantata* with an instrumental accompaniment. Often associated with Christmas. Spanish, seventeenth century. **3.** A Christmas carol.
villanella (It),	A rustic song or instrumental piece.
villanelle (F)	
vina	An Indian string instrument of the *lute* variety.
vinyl, vinyl disc	Disc used for analog recording playback machines during the second half of the last century. Usually made in black vinyl plastic.
viola	Alto member of the violin family, with four strings tuned to C,G,D,A. Played under the chin.
viola da braccio (It)	'Arm viol'. The tenor viol, played held on the arm.
viola da gamba (It)	'Leg viol'. The bass viol, played held between the knees.
viola d'amore (It)	'Love viol'. Tenor instrument of the *viol family*, with seven strings, and seven to fourteen sympathetic strings.
violão (P)	*Guitar*.
violeiro (P)	Brazilian guitarist, especially *troubadour* of rural Brazil.
violento,	Violent, violently.
violentamente (It)	
violenza (It)	Violence.
viol family	A family of bowed instruments from the sixteenth and seventeenth centuries. With flat back, frets and six strings, the common sizes were treble, tenor and bass.
violin	Bowed four-string instrument, the principal member of the family of instruments known as the violin family, which emerged at the beginning of the sixteenth century.
Violine (G), **violino,**	*Violin*, violins.
violini (It)	

violino (P)	*Violin.*
Violinschlüssel (G)	*Treble clef.*
violon (F)	*Violin.*
violoncelle (F)	*Cello.*
violoncello	*Cello.* Bowed four-string instrument of the violin family.
violone (It)	Big viol.
	1. A double bass sized *viol*.
	2. A *double bass*.
	3. In Italian *Baroque* music, a *cello*.
virada (P)	Change in percussion pattern.
virelai	Type of medieval French song, with a repeating *refrain*.
virginal(s)	Keyboard instrument of the *harpsichord* family.
virtuoso (It)	Performer with outstanding technical skill.
vite, vitement (F)	Quick, quickly.
vivace, vivo (It)	Lively.
vivamente (It)	In lively fashion.
vivezza (It)	Life.
vivido (It)	Vivacious.
vivo (It)	Lively.
vocalese	A style of jazz singing where the melody is taken from a previously improvised instrumental solo, and words are added.
vocalise (F)	*Vocalize.*
vocalize	To sing on a vowel, with decorative or emotional effect.
vocalizzo (It)	*Vocalize.*
vocal score	*Score* with voice parts, usually arranged for piano accompaniment.
voce, voci (It)	Voice, voices.
vocoder	**VO**ice en**CODER**. In *synthesis*, combining the profile of speech with the pitch and tonal characteristics of music. Thus a piano could be made to seem to talk, as in Sparky's Magic Piano.
voglia (It)	Longing.
voice-leading	*Part-writing.* The direction an individual inner voice takes in *polyphonic* harmonic writing.
voice-over	A soundtrack containing a commentary or announcement to accompany pictures, but with the speaker off camera.
voicing	**1.** The vertical arrangement of parts in an ensemble.

2. Adjustment for tone quality, in organs by adjusting the pipes, in pianos by adjusting the hammers.

voilé (F)	Veiled.
voix (F)	Voice.
volante (It)	Flying.
Volkslied (G)	*Folk song.*
Volksliedermelodie, Volksweise (G)	Folk song melody, folk tune.
Volkston (G)	Folk style.
voll (G)	Full.
volles Werk (G)	Full organ.
völlig (G)	Complete.
volltönig, volltönend (G)	Full-sounding. Sonorous.
volonté, à (F)	Performed freely.
volti, volti subito (It)	Turn, turn the page quickly.
volubile, volubilmente (It)	Voluble, flowing easily.
volume	Loudness.
voluntary	An organ solo, often improvised, placed at the beginning or end of a church service.
von (G)	From.
von hier (G)	From here.
vor (G)	Before, in front of, ago.
vorbereiten (G)	To prepare.
Vorbühne (G)	Apron stage.
vorgetragen (G)	Brought out, prominent.
Vorhalt (G)	1. *Suspension.*
	2. *Retardation.*
	3. Long *appoggiatura.*
	4. *Syncopation.*
Vorhang (G)	Curtain.
Vorhang nehmen (G)	To take a curtain call.
vorher, vorherig (G)	Before, previously.
Vorschlag (G)	Forestroke. *Appoggiatura.*
vorsingen (G)	To sing in front of someone.
Vorspiel (G)	*Prelude. Overture.*
vorspielen (G)	To *audition.*
Vorspieler (G)	Court pianist.
Vorstellung (G)	Performance.
vortragen, vorzutragen (G)	To perform, to bring forward prominently.
vorwärts (G)	Forwards.

vox (L)

V.S.

vuoto, vuota (It)

Voice.

Abbreviation of *volti subito*, turn (the page) quickly.

'Empty'. Applied to a measure of music in which all performers have a rest, or, as in *corda vuota*, an empty string, i.e. open.

W

wachsend (G)
Growing. *Crescendo.*

Wachtelpfeife (G)
Quailpipe.

Wagner tuba
Five-valved horns, with funnel-shaped mouth pieces. Designed to a specification by Richard Wagner (1813-1883) for use in Der Ring des Nibelungen, and more like a modified orchestral horn than the normal tuba.

während (G)
During.

waist
The narrowing of the middle of the body of a string instrument, designed in part to allow movement of the bow, or to facilitate holding the instrument.

waits
1. Medieval guards who sounded the hours on musical instruments.
2. Old English name for the *shawm*, an instrument frequently used by the waits.

Waldhorn (G)
Forest horn. Hunting horn. A natural horn, the eighteenth century antecedent of the modern *French horn.*

walk, walking bass
A bass line of steady quarter notes.

Walkman
A small portable tape recorder, created by the Japanese Sony corporation in 1981.

waltz (Eng),
Walzer (G), **valse** (F)
Dance in triple time which enjoyed great popularity in the nineteenth century.

Walze (G)
Crescendo pedal on the organ.

Waltzer tanzen (G)
To waltz.

Wärme (G)
Warmth.

washboard
A laundry board, with a corrugated wood or metal surface, played with wire brushes or metal thimbles. Used in early *jazz* and English *skiffle.*

wassail
A word that frequently occurs in Christmas carols. A festive event, with drinking.

water organ
An ancient Greek or Roman instrument. A hydraulic organ without bellows, which is blown by air that is compressed by water.

waveform
In *synthesis*, the shape of a sound when viewed on an oscilloscope. It determines the timbre of the sound.

wa-wa (wah-wah)
1. On brass instruments, a 'wah' sound produced by covering and uncovering the bell (or sometimes the stem of a *Harmon* mute inserted into the bell), using a *cup* mute or *plunger* mute.

2. On electric guitars, a 'wah' sound produced by sweeping a resonant filter up and down the frequency spectrum.

wechseln (G) — To change.

weg (G) — Away. Off.

wehmütig (G) — Sad.

weich (G) — Soft. Gentle.

Weihnachtslied, Weihnachtslieder (G) — Christmas carol, Christmas carols.

weinend (G) — Wailing. Weeping.

Weinlied (G) — Wine song. Drinking song.

Weise (G) — Way, manner, melody.

wenig (G) — Little.

werdend (G) — Becoming.

stärker werdend (G) — Becoming louder.

Werk, Werke (G) — Work, works. Compositions.

West Coast style — Type of American modern jazz played in California during the 1950s.

whammy bar — A guitar device that moves the *bridge*, changing the pitch of the strings.

whip — A percussion instrument imitative of a whipcrack. Two flat pieces of wood are joined by a hinge into a V-shape, and are snapped together to make the sound.

whistle — **1.** Simple end-blown *flute*.
2. Human sound made by puckering the lips and blowing.

white label — A small-scale production of a record or *CD*, with an anonymous blank (hence 'white') label.

white noise — Just as white light contains all the colors in the visual spectrum, white noise contains all audio frequencies in the aural spectrum.

whizzer — *Thunder stick.*

whole note — Semibreve.

whole step — Two semitones.

whole tone — Two semitones.

whole tone scale — A six note *scale* comprised solely of *whole steps*, with no semitones.

widerhallen (G) — To resound.

wie (G) — As.

wie am Anfang (G) — As at the beginning.

wieder (G) — Again.

wiederholen (G) — To repeat.

wiegen (G)	To rock.
Wiegenlied (G)	*Lullaby.*
wind band	Large wind ensemble with percussion, also known as *concert band, marching band* or *military band.*
wind chimes	Instrument more for domestic decoration than for performance. Varied lengths of cane, metal or wood, suspended from a frame, and sounded by the wind, or by striking.
wind instrument	Any instrument sounded by the player's breath. Includes *woodwind* and *brass.*
wind machine	A machine used in the theater to imitate the sound of the wind, usually by cranking a large cylinder over which is draped and tensioned a heavy fabric such as canvas.
windshield	Cover to protect microphone from wind noise. See *pop cover.*
Wirbel (G)	Literally 'whirl'. Drum-*roll.* Also tuning *peg.*
wire brush	A type of drumstick with a head of many stiff springy wires.
wohlgefällig (G)	Pleasant. Pleasantly.
wohltemperiert (G)	Well-tempered. Equal tempered.
wolf, wolf tone	Strident unwanted note.
wood block	Hollowed hardwood block, played with a stick. Frequently part of the kit of a dance band, jazz or rock drummer.
woodwind	Instruments that are blown, but in which the vibrating agent is *not* the lips. The family includes *flute, oboe, clarinet, bassoon* and *saxophone.* Formerly most of these (except the *saxophone*) were made of wood.
work song	A rhythmic song used to coordinate any type of gang work.
world music	Non-mainstream music, usually foreign and of a *folk* type. Also *global music.* An imprecise term.
wow	Unintentional changes of pitch in sound reproduction equipment.
wuchtig (G)	Weighty. Powerful.
Wunsch (G)	Wish.
nach Wunsch (G)	*Ad lib.,* freely.
würdig (G)	Worthy. Dignified.
Wurlitzer	American firm of organ builders.
Wurstfagott (G)	Sausage *bassoon. Racket, cervelas.*
Wut (G)	Temper. Fury.
wütend (G)	Furious.

X

x	Muted struck string in guitar *tablature*.
xácara, jácara	An old Spanish song-dance.
xaxado (P)	Song and dance from northeastern Brazil.
xerém (P)	Song and dance from northeastern Brazil.
xique-xique (P)	Type of *chocalho*. Type of cactus.
xocalho (P)	*Chocalho*.
xote (P)	Dance from northeastern Brazil. Derived from the *Schottische*.
Xylophon (G)	*Xylophone*.
xylophone	Percussion instrument with tuned horizontal wooden bars laid out in the pattern of piano keys. The bars are played with beaters or mallets.
xylorimba	Tuned percussion instrument, combining the range of *xylophone* and *marimba*.

Y

yodel

A type of singing for men, particularly in the Swiss and Austrian Alpine region. Features a rapid alternation between natural voice and *falsetto*. The music is usually very simple, leading one writer to describe it as 'more a sport than an art form'.

Z

Z	Abbreviation for Franklin B. Zimmerman, the American musicologist who compiled the catalog of the works of Henry Purcell.
zabumba (P)	Type of Brazilian bass drum.
zählen (G)	To count.
Zählzeit (G)	'Count-time'. Beat.
zambra	Spanish dance with Moorish influence.
zapateado	Spanish solo dance, vigorous in nature, with stamping.
zart (G)	Tender, delicate.
zarzuela	Traditional Spanish stage entertainment with music and spoken dialogue.
Zäsur (G)	Break, pause.
zehn (G)	Ten.
Zeichen (G)	Sign.
Zeit (G)	Time.
sich **Zeit lassen** (G)	To take one's time.
zeitgenössisch (G)	Contemporary.
Zeitmass, Zeitmaß (G)	Tempo.
zelo, zeloso,	Zeal, zealously.
zelosamente (It)	
ziehen (G)	To draw out.
Ziehharmonika (G)	*Accordion.*
ziemlich (G)	Rather, quite.
zierlich (G)	Elegant.
Zigeuner,	Gypsy, gypsy music.
Zigeunermusik (G)	
zimbalon	*Dulcimer.*
zingaro, zingara (It)	Gypsy.
Zink (G)	*Cornett* (keyed bugle).
Zither (G)	*Zither.*
zither	Flat-backed string instrument laid on the knees or on a table. The strings run the length of the body. *Autoharp, dulcimer, Hackbrett, koto, psaltery,* are all part of the family.
zitternd (G)	Trembling.
zögernd (G)	Delaying. Same as *rallentando.*
zone	An area on a synthesizer keyboard that controls a specific set of functions.
zoppa (It)	Lame. Syncopated. *Alla zoppa* is the same as *Scots snap.*

zortzico	Basque folk dance with five beats in a measure.
zu (G)	To, too.
zuerst (G)	First, at first.
Züge (G)	*Flies* (theatrical).
Zugposaune (G)	Slide trombone.
Zuhörer (G)	Listener, audience.
zum Anfang (G)	To the beginning.
zunehmend (G)	Increasing.
Zunge (G)	Tongue, *reed.*
zupfen (G)	To pluck.
zurück (G)	Back.
zurückhalten (G)	To hold back.
zurücktreten (G)	To step back.
zusammen (G)	Together.
Zuschauer (G)	Audience, spectator.
Zuschauerraum (G)	Auditorium.
zutraulich (G)	Confidingly, intimately.
zuvor (G)	Before.
zwei (G)	Two.
zweimal (G)	Twice.
zweite, zweites (G)	Second.
zweiter Rang (G)	Upper circle.
Zweiunddreissigstel,	Demisemiquaver, thirty-second note.
Zweiunddreißigstel (G)	
zwischen (G)	Between.
Zwischenspiel (G)	*Interlude, episode* in a *fugue.*
zwölf (G)	Twelve.
Zwölftonmusik,	*Twelve-note* music, *twelve-tone* or *dodecaphonic*
Zwölftontechnik (G)	music.
zydeco	Afro-American dance music of Southern Louisiana. The name is alleged to come from the *Creole* pronunciation of 'les haricots' ('zarico). Regarded as the Afro-American equivalent of *Cajun*.
Zyklus (G)	Cycle. Also *Cyklus*.
zymbalum	Same as *zimbalon*.

Notes

Notes

EXCELLENCE IN MUSIC